To Pete,

Wishing you a very happy birthday.

I spent many a happy day pottering around the Fens with John Humphreys. I hope you enjoy it.

Warmest regards,

Roger

Country Gun

John Humphreys

COUNTRYMAN, AUTHOR, NATURALIST

Country Gun

John Humphreys

COUNTRYMAN, AUTHOR, NATURALIST

Quiller

Copyright © 2012 John Humphreys

First published in the UK in 2012
by Quiller, an imprint of Quiller Publishing Ltd

British Library Cataloguing-in-Publication Data
A catalogue record for this book
is available from the British Library

ISBN 978 1 84689 175 5

The right of John Humphreys to be identified as the author of this work
has been asserted in accordance with the Copyright, Design and Patent
Act 1988

Book and jacket design by Sharyn Troughton
Printed in Malta by Gutenberg Press Ltd

Quiller

An imprint of Quiller Publishing Ltd
Wykey House, Wykey, Shrewsbury, SY4 1JA
Tel: 01939 261616 Fax: 01939 261606
E-mail: info@quillerbooks.com
Website: www.countrybooksdirect.

Contents

Introduction

*Sitting on his bench in his favourite place on earth –
Hunter's Fen – a few weeks before his death in
February 2012, John Humphreys told me
the story of the eight acres of forgotten
marsh, just a stone's throw from Cambridge,
which he had reclaimed for the benefit of
nature and the odd day's shooting.*

T he story of Hunter's Fen is a fascinating one and as a storyteller John was unsurpassed. To be with him as he recounted the history of every plant, reed, and splash and the tales of the visiting wildlife on the small patch he had lovingly nurtured was a privilege I cherish – but it is also a privilege that has been enjoyed by thousands. John was an unfailingly generous man when it came to sharing his passion for the countryside and the country sports he lived for. Thanks both to his writing and to his companionable nature, several generations of countrymen and women shared his delight in the life he enjoyed, whether it was with rod, gun or a carefully tended sapling in hand. Many, including thousands who had never even met him, considered him their friend and a champion of their way of life.

For 40 years, John Humphreys wrote regularly for *Shooting Times*, producing sufficient copy to fill a bible several times over. Born in 1939, he enjoyed a childhood in the fens that gave him the freedom to roam about the landscape he so cherished. From an early age he was a loyal reader of the magazine he later became so closely associated with. His father, Canon of Ely cathedral and vicar in a small Cambridgeshire village, deemed it highly suitable reading matter for a young boy with an insuppressible love of the outdoors and the natural world, and generously agreed to cover the cost of the weekly purchase. John's relationship with the magazine was one that grew stronger later in his life when, in 1972, he realised his dream and saw his first article appear in print.

Writing as 'Fenman', an enthusiastic response from readers meant that, steadily, his work appeared more and more frequently. In time, a column by John was an essential feature of *Shooting Times* every week, where his writing appeared under the more appropriate heading of 'Country Gun', a title which perfectly described the duality of his approach to the British landscape. For him, shooting and conservation of the natural world were inextricably linked, a fact that was recognised in 1995 when he received, from HRH The Prince of Wales, a Laurent Perrier Award for Game and Conservation for his work on the Lord's Ground shoot, the small, friendly local shoot that still meets regularly throughout the season close to Hunter's Fen.

What was it about John and his writing that generated such a following? He was first and foremost an outdoorsman, through and through. One of his most formative experiences was when, in his teens, he met Dr Eric Ennion on a bird-ringing holiday in Northumberland. Ennion, a renowned ornithologist and artist, became a mentor to the young naturalist, helping to instil a rich understanding of nature that John transferred so captivatingly into his prose. John's subsequent career as a teacher was the perfect outlet for his desire to inspire, explain and nurture, traits which come through strongly in his writing.

John's open-heartedness meant that he made friends wherever he went. This aspect of his character meant he was lucky enough to have access to a vast array of experiences and, consequently, a vast catalogue of stories to tell, whether it was grouse shooting with dukes on the finest moors in his later years, or partaking in some altogether more dubious shooting as a youngster with the sexton's dodgy hammergun strapped across the front of his bicycle. When it came to storytelling, he was equally capable of captivating an audience of grizzled wildfowlers as he was the local WI with tales of the marsh. A multi-talented man, he could even keep them entertained with an impromptu virtuoso Dixieland jazz solo. He took most situations in his stride and always found some aspect of his adventures that was sure to enthral his keen readers.

In addition to his regular writing for *Shooting Times*, John wrote frequently for *Country Life* and *The Field* and produced more than 20 books on the countryside and country sports, including highly regarded works such as *Poachers' Tales, The Countryman's Year* and *Hunter's Fen.* He was prolific and his success was down to the manner in which he treated his readers. He wrote directly for them. His writing is clever, but not in an artful or sharp way. John's skill was in bringing the reader on-side using a great deal of wit and self-deprecating humour, an encyclopaedic knowledge of his subject and a conversational style.

In selecting what to include in this book, John's wife, Angela, and I realised that there were clear divisions in John's work that reflect where his principal interests lay. He made his name as a master of the sporting tale, so, as you would expect, there is a section dedicated to his writing on shooting sports both at home and abroad. Similarly, friends and family were of huge importance to John in his writing, and this is shown in the fact that there is a section devoted to sporting tales that feature those he loved the most.

The first time I witnessed the queue of people coming to chat with John on the *Shooting Times* stand at that annual pilgrimage for all things country – the CLA Game Fair – I came to appreciate that here was a man who was both widely known and widely loved. Part of the reason he was so widely known was because he enjoyed incorporating many of these sporting characters into his writing. Part of the reason he was so widely loved was because he never did so in a malicious or vinegary way. John was fascinated by other people's stories, and a section on these characters was an inevitability.

Amongst his strongest writing was certainly that on natural history, and it was a painless task to fill a section with the best of his articles on such a wide subject that beguiled him, including, notably, a number of the superb pieces he wrote later in his life for *Country Life*.

This anthology would not be complete without including some of John's finest writing on fishing. For him, if you could not be out shooting, then you could certainly be out casting a line. One of his proudest moments was the day on which three generations of his family caught salmon on the Tweed – the Country Gun column of that day is here in the mix.

Although later in his life John had the opportunity to travel the globe – and many pieces on his adventures are featured here – it was his home turf that was most important to him. The fens held a special magic and much of his writing relayed that to his readers. John's work would not be reflected accurately if it did not include a section devoted to the landscape he so adored.

Finally, there is a section dedicated to the young sportsman. Tirelessly John fostered the next generation of shooters and naturalists, seeking to endow them with a love of the world as he saw it. He held a strong sense that we are merely temporary custodians of the world around us. He often used to cite the proverb that 'Men plant trees that their sons may sit in the shade'. It made it into his articles on several occasions. He liked the sentiment and it is one that he endorsed both in writing and physically in the landscape that he so enjoyed managing near his home. John also had a good eye for a bargain and recognised the tremendous value that could be had from the purchase of one cheap Spanish 20-bore, bought for his sons and passed on to countless others taking their first steps in the shooting world. For him, the return on that investment alone was incalculable.

It has been my pleasure to help select pieces for inclusion in this book, in honour of a man whose life touched thousands. Having worked on *Shooting Times* and known John for the past decade, one thing that surprised me was quite how clearly I could recall all the pieces he had written when looking back at them. Many of the stories, even from many years ago, came rushing to the front of my mind. Casting through his work with the help of Angela, many pieces made me smile immediately with the recollection, as I hope they will make you smile also, whether you are coming to them fresh or have followed John in writing for years.

I would like to thank four people for their help in compiling this book: firstly, Jane Watkins and Mark Hedges, chief sub-editor and editor respectively, for their help with articles of John's from *Country Life*. Mark was a good friend of John's from his own period as editor on *Shooting Times* and his advice and support has been invaluable. Katharina Doyle, the lynchpin of the editorial office at *Shooting Times*, shared with me the task of preparing much of the earlier (pre-computer era) copy and her input has been enormous. Finally, I'd like to thank Angela Humphreys for her considerable help in finding the best pieces from a lifetime of exceptional work. I trust that this book is a fitting tribute to her husband's memory.

Alastair Balmain
Editor, *Shooting Times*

September 2012

Sporting Tales

From pigeon to grouse, John Humphreys enjoyed a truly rich and varied shooting career. The pieces in this chapter illustrate both his attitude to the sport he loved and the variety of sport he enjoyed throughout his life.

In the beginning, 9 January 1992

Pottering is the root of all field shooting from which all others originated.
In this Country Gun column from early 1992, John describes the type of
sport that formed the bedrock of his shooting life.

Most of us start our shooting lives by pottering around, and here lies the root and branch of all field shooting. Today it is harder to find such land than when I was an 'old boy', for much 'potterable' ground has been 'taken in hand', and its capacity to show great numbers of indifferent, reared birds and make lots of money for its owner has been fully exploited. However, with the proliferation of that peculiar lunacy set aside, and due to the recession and the failing of the more blatantly commercial reared bird shoots, land for pottering is becoming available once more.

Your average potterer must have a considerable acreage of non-prolific land and carry a basic minimum of equipment, for he might walk some miles during a good potter. There again, he might be through and done within an hour. That is part of the beauty of it: there is nothing set in concrete, with decisions and tactics made and broken at a whim. If there is a shift in the wind or a sudden shower, you try plan B, then C, D and so on until you run out of letters and have to start again. A capacious bag is essential, and somewhere in the old feathers and empty cases at the bottom, you should have a lead weight on a cord, which is vital for unblocking your gun barrel. You may need it only once in a decade but on that day it will save your sport.

A potterer cannot function without a dog. It need not be a field trial champion, but it should have no fear of working dense cover. It should also be good in water, a reliable retriever, a cheerful companion and, in the case of potterers of advancing years, not too swift on its feet. I am a Labrador man, but the dog with the qualifications for this job is the English springer spaniel.

The potterer starts in the farmyard and sets off to quarter the acres, as did the beaver-hatted gents of the 18th century with their long, brown guns, flint and steel, in the days when every straggly stubble field held three good coveys of grey partridge. Today that bird is less likely to be on the list as the pheasant tends to dominate, but the chance of a rabbit, hare, pigeon, snipe, woodcock, mallard or teal adds the spice of the unexpected.

There is no helpful keeper to carry the bag, no host to dictate to you what will happen next, no beaters to witness the hits and misses – just you and a good companion.

Down on the Bedford Washes I disturbed a pheasant somewhere in the second field away from home in a post Christmas potter. Accompanied by a palsied but wily old Labrador, we set off on the line, plodding along in leisurely fashion. A pheasant here was a thing to be prized, an opportunity not to be squandered.

The bird crossed one field and then turned along a dyke choked with reeds. This seemed a good place for it to have tucked in, but no, it was off again, down to the end, quickly across a splashy bit of flooding and into the Norfolk reeds beyond. Here we had a delay but old Ajax, thrown for a moment, picked up the point where the bird had stopped before moving out into the tussocky grass beyond. There was no rush, no sense of urgency, but a stolid and relentless plodding on, bearing to the left, then to the right, sometimes backtracking for a while, just following the scent of what hunting folk would call the 'pilot', time no object, distance of no importance.

A cormorant beat overhead, a moorhen spattered across a dyke and had me twitching, while a skein of greylags flew over, star high, as steady as a constellation. The denouement came at last. The old dog grew animated, his tail aflail as he bustled around in a stand of sedge. The world stood still and then, with an eruption of wings, a glorious cock pheasant sprang aloft with a throaty chortle. Giving him due law I would, with a bit of luck, undo following wind, drop him dead, admire his plumage, get my bearings and plod off again for another – though one was enough.

That was 40 years ago and I did much the same this very day – lots of *déjà vu*, for little had changed. Along with No. 2 son and his friend we tramped the dykes, a new dog working and bustling, a fen pheasant less of a rarity but the skills of decision-making, minor tactics and old-fashioned hunting unchanged.

We took a long reed-choked dyke far into the misty distance, just the place for a pheasant on a cold and windy day. This late in the year the birds have mastered the art of hiding, but we arrived back at the car two hours later with glowing cheeks, all signs of festive excess blown clean away – plus three cock pheasants, two moorhen, two pigeon, a hare and a teal. The shot of the day was one of the moorhens, high and blown like a bat by the stiffening gale it came hurtling over.

Finally it was down to the pond to await the mallard. I took the 8-bore to give Peter his first feel of heavy metal. My home loads, 2½oz of 3s and six drams of fine grain black powder – a combination designed for me years ago by Homeloader for use in the Remington industrial cases – had proved strong medicine in the double Patstone underlever, a gun middle-aged when Queen Victoria died. We waited, and in the end three birds swung round. A 12-bore cracked and a bird fell, but to dwarf such a pathetic squib came an awesome boom, a great squirt of sparks, flame and a float of acrid black powder smoke. The earth trembled, but the bird carried on.

Two shots later it happened. Again there came the Krakatoa eruption, but this time the aim was true and a mallard balled in mid-air, hitting the centre of the pond with the emphasis of a depth charge. Then Trevor, at the end, wanted a go. His mallard was not at unhittable range, being some eight yards at a guess, but he had no time to change guns. The majestic explosion had the roosting pheasants complaining and the flame from the muzzle seemed to scorch the very breast of the incoming duck. "Would you like that one for soup?" someone shouted.

When covert shoots have gone to dust, regulated out of existence through some EC or domestic piece of nonsense, the potterer will survive, for his is the original sport from which the rest sprang. The meek will inherit the earth.

Winter pigeon, 30 December 1982

Although in season other quarry often took precedence, pigeon shooting still had a strong appeal to John – so much so that he wrote several books on the subject. In this Country Gun column from 1982 he recounts a rare December day in the hide.

The schoolteacher who shoots, not, one hopes, at his pupils, but at more sporting targets, finds that his activities' needs must be concentrated into certain periods. Autumn term begins in early September, just time for some early mallard, and then marches on to the end of October when we have a week into which too many things have to be crammed. Then there is the long pull until Christmas and another all too short cessation of hostilities. In my own case, every Saturday from mid-August until 1 February is taken up mostly with shooting but also with some picking-up. I am not complaining, and count my blessings, but the rhythm of the professional year is such that mid-week shooting must be concentrated into two periods, late October and three weeks at Christmas.

One does not wish to waste these precious days, and kind friends who shoot mid-week are generous enough to try and squeeze me in at these times, but it does mean that I miss out on a number of marvellous days. Friends in other lines of work who take their holidays as they wish can, unlike the teacher, take a day off for a special occasion. Shooting time must be carefully husbanded and in a series of straight value judgements, with which I would be surprised if everyone agreed, I put wildfowling above pike fishing, snipe shooting above amateur keepering and game shooting above pigeon shooting – all purely personal but reluctant choices for there are only so many hours available each week. This does not mean that the second choices are eliminated completely but one can pursue only one quarry at a time. Just now and then a break occurs, an unexpected gap in the tight schedule caused for one of many reasons, but it means a chance to enjoy a minor foray after quarry usually pursued in less busy times of the year.

It was a curious and tragic circumstance which gave me a day 'off'.

The pheasant shoot I was due to attend as a guest, a likely 300-bird day, was cancelled due to a sudden bereavement. I found myself with a spare day on my hands and, lo and behold, that trickle of pigeon I had observed loping over the thorns and onto the chickweed in an old stubble, moved from the corner of my eye and mind to the focus point of my attention.

At any other time of the year, away from the cream of the shooting season, I would have seized such a chance. Now it was too late even to arrange some picking-up and the duck would not drop into the wash in the still air of this early December evening, so the pigeon it had to be.

There are advantages and drawbacks to pigeon shooting in winter. In some ways the sport is more like wildfowling as, growing colder by the minute, you crouch in a hide. It is a far cry from lounging indolently in the shade of an elder bush by a stubble on a bee-buzzing August afternoon. You will need to wrap up well, with plenty of layers of warm clothes, a handwarmer or two, balaclava helmet and other Arctic wear. Waiting in a hide, trying to keep still for a long period means that the body heat gradually leaks away and a cold shooter is ever a bad shooter. It may become necessary, during a lull, to come out of the hide and stamp up and down, violently flapping the arms in order to restore the circulation.

Another difference is the hide. The usual dark green and brown camouflage netting is far too conspicuous against the bleached grass and generally pale hues of winter and there is a shortage of foliage and natural materials to make a natural hide. A patchwork quilt of old sacks, bundles of dead sticks or, best of all, my pale brown 'stocking hide' will, by the imaginative, be pressed into service. Sparse vegetation also means that your static, ground decoys will show up proudly, but it is worth remembering that on snow, heavy hoar frost or on tall kale or rape, decoys do not seem easily to be seen by pigeon eyes: even a wing-flapper loses its magic.

On the credit side, you will be one of the few decoyers out: the rest of them will be snug indoors or out in pursuit of what they consider to be nobler quarry. Also, the birds will tend to be more hungry and will feed hard during the short hours of daylight. I write now of pigeon which are not suffering from a long spell of snow and frost when the food supply is locked away and they quickly lose condition. In fact, pigeon in early winter are often in surprisingly good trim and as fat as butter.

Bearing my own advice in mind, I muffled myself heavily in layers of quilted coats until I resembled one, if not both, of the Michelin twins: it was not ideal for swift shooting, but at least I would not suffer from exposure. Lover as I am of the English countryside in all its moods, a dank December day is not the time to see it at its best. Just for once I fell prey to the guilty thought that, were I a man of means, I would summon up my private helicopter, float out to the nearest airport and, with a clean shirt and a toothbrush as luggage, jet out to some remote sub-tropical spot. Wishful thinking comes easily with a 50lb rucksack on your back and the icy sludge of Fen mud creeping further up your boots with every step. It was not to be, and no magic chopper came whirring down to whisk me away to the sunshine.

I pushed such traitorous thoughts to the back of my mind and set up a squad of 20 HH decoys on the old stubble, 20 yards from a thick thorn hedge. I chopped away at some dead hawthorn, getting well pricked for my troubles, but I managed to erect a rough thorn boma, or truncated wigwam which I clad in a skirt made of my lightest shade of hide netting. Getting it off again at the end took rather longer. Seated comfortably therein, I pulled my drapes firmly about me and gazed out at my 'picture'. Three pheasants came out from the stand of maize on the next field and strutted about. The dreary gloom of the winter day had turned even the cock's glorious colours to drab fustian.

Then, wondrous to relate, a pigeon came and settled on the ash tree, 30 yards away. Recalling the advice I first read in a Min of Ag pamphlet back in the '50s, I took careful aim at its feet and fired the choke barrel. Having followed this advice regularly for 30 years, I knew exactly what to expect, so I was not surprised when the bird went clattering away, apparently untouched, to fly strongly away across the river and out of sight.

My peripheral vision of earlier weeks had not played me false, for birds did start dropping in, circling high above like wheeling buzzards in diminishing circles – one moment dots in the sky and the next hovering over the decoys. These hoverers can be as hard to hit as birds sitting in ash trees, but my blood was up – cold, but up – and I got the first five without a miss. Then a flock came and three fell out; too good to be true and I counted my blessings and my birds as I restored my circulation by scampering out to set them up.

The rest of the afternoon was a miracle, a recollection of a good day back in the '50s when the ill-advised pamphlet was written. Birds came in boldly in a steady trickle and while my opening average was far too good to last, I killed more than I missed, ending the day with 62 birds in the bag and a quiet glow of pride in my thermolactycally encased bosom.

When it was all over, I trudged back to the homes of civilised men and a warming dram with all thoughts of tropical climes and suchlike nonsense vanished like a summer mist.

The Sporting Moor, 12 August 1982

Although his readers closely associated him with the Cambridgeshire fens, for many years, John was part of a syndicate that leased the shooting on a small grouse moor in the Pennines. Here he describes the joy of working, and walking, for your sport.

The Londoner rarely goes to visit The Tower: the Cambridge man hurries daily past the glories of King's College Chapel, his eyes on the pavement and his thoughts on the trivia of his own affairs. It is left to strangers, travellers of sometimes thousands of miles, to come and gape at these wonders, to buy the guide books and end the day better versed in our treasures than we are ourselves, after a lifetime next door to them. Familiarity breeds contempt and being near a thing makes us careless of its value.

To the lowland gunner, grouse and geese, by their distance from his regular haunts, assume potent properties. He drives many miles north in pursuit of them. On the way he passes northerners driving the other way in search of the pheasants and partridges he left behind. The mountain shooter must dream of chirruping coveys and rocketing pheasants as I dream of the grey battalions and red grouse springing chuckling from the purple heather. As the summer begins to grow stale, the Game Fair is over and the combines are gobbling up the last swathes of winter wheat, grouse thoughts disturb my sleep increasingly.

I am lucky to have a gun in a walking moor of about 4,000 acres of grass and heather on the top of the Pennines. It is beautiful country, benign on balmy summer days, but cruel and unrelenting when the cold rain swirls up the gullies and stings your face red raw. To say that the moor is not swarming with grouse and to add that a total season's bag might equal that of a fair-to-average day on one of the 'posh' moors would be no less than the truth, but it would be to state an irrelevance and to miss the whole point of our outings there.

Every single bird of that 100 brace, spread over a series of long weekends from mid-August until the end of September, provides a deal of pleasure to the Guns, guests, friends, walkers and children who make the pilgrimage year after year and who make up the shooting parties. Our birds are appreciated, every one an adventure, a treasured moment, carefully recollected in subsequent tranquility. The physical effort involved in plodding up those endless inclines and floundering in the peat hags, makes every bird bagged by us effete southerners a triumph of mind over matter.

The hub, around which our activities revolve, is the substantial stone cottage which goes with the moor and where many a mighty breakfast is eaten, jolly evening spent, many a bottle has been broached there and nights have been passed putting the shooting world to rights. Despite its small size, over 20 people have slept there, more or less comfortably (snorers in the dining room), while more than a dozen dogs have whined or growled the night away in the hay loft. It has been a place of such happy occasions that it has come to hold a special niche in the affections of those who have come to know it well.

Another feature of having a gun on a grouse moor, even quite a modest one like this, is the pure luxury of shooting birds which, apart from the immediate strains of pursuit, you have not earned. Readers may be aware that I believe in building up my own sport; putting back into the countryside some of what I take out and, by improving the game stocks, tidying up and enhancing the land. Cover planting, feeding and vermin control plus the keeper's foot on the soil are the usual paths to these ends but the grouse moor is a sort of legalised poaching, for I lift not a finger to protect the birds in hard times, but take so much out for so little put in. The place is keepered in a casual sort of way but there is no heather burning or gritting which, together with crow and fox control, are about all you can do to help grouse.

In the rare moments when this thought intrudes, I console myself with the reflection that grouse have managed quite well on their own, and the shooting of over-populations is one of the best things we can do to help them. Grouse left without a territory by Christmas have scant chance of survival but are chivvied from place to place as they search for food until they die. As a species they are susceptible to numerous parasites; a current Game Conservancy project is researching the effects upon them of the sheep tick. It is not unusual, as you tramp along, to find the remains of a dead one.

Peregrines, owls, harriers, foxes and crows all take their share. Grouse inhabit some of the most inhospitable parts of the British Isles. Heavy snow and poor breeding seasons are facts of life to them. Only last year our moor was under ten feet of snow in April, the middle of nesting time, but, in spite of this, they managed a moderate hatch. They are easy birds to kill, for a single pellet is often enough to bring one down.

Beset by enemies within and without, living in beautiful but harsh and cruel places, existing by uncompromising laws of survival of the fittest, the grouse still seem to thrive. They have their good and bad years but they are always there and, barring some cataclysmic disaster, are likely to remain so.

Grouse may be easy to kill, but they are by no means easy to hit. Experienced sportsmen have named as one of the most testing birds, the late-season driven grouse, skimming round the contours and zipping over the butts with the wind in its tail. Our moor is, as I have said, mostly walking, but we do have two places where a drive is possible. One is a line of dilapidated butts, the other a deep gully running up the hill with a drystone wall at right angles to it at the top. In these butts I killed my first ever grouse, a single bird which flew along the line and which, to our mutual surprise, fell with a puff of white feathers into the bents by the ghyll. Thus was my name added to the long list, since grown much longer, of those lucky people who have killed their first grouse in this happy place.

Another of the delights is the company, generous sportsmen and kindly people all. One incident will serve to make the point. One autumn day we were toiling along as usual when a single blackcock sprang whirring out of the blaeberries. Trevor, at the far end of the line, fired; the bird staggered, flew on strongly and, when it was a distant dot, towered and fell. Blackgame are rare on the moor, and this was the first and last of the year; it was also Trevor's first blackcock so could not be left. Two dog men went to search the featureless ground, two hills away over the horizon, where we had marked it down. The terrain was wet, knee-high bents; scent was poor. Trevor protested we leave the bird and waste no one's time, but two Guns, one a guest – there for his first day – and the other the shoot captain, gave up the rest of the morning and all of the afternoon in searching every inch of that ground while the rest of us pushed on. No one could have blamed them had they abandoned the hunt after an hour or so, but, just as hope was fading, their pertinacity was rewarded for Vince's huge, leonine yellow Labrador, Rob, found it. The bird was laid out on the cool slabs in the yard when the rest of us returned to base that evening, while the two radiant searchers, bathed and shaved, halos glowing, were enjoying a gin and tonic, The fact that it was also Trevor's birthday gave the subsequent celebrations an added zest.

This is the spirit in which all shooting ought to be conducted. You come to appreciate the real meaning of the word sportsmanship by enjoying each unpredictable aspect of such sport as and when it comes along, rather than rushing about in a relentless pursuit of bigger and bigger bags and the ruinous competitive itch to which Man is prone. The high tops, the grouse, the company, the guiding spirit, the cottage and the sense of adventure make, for all of us, a wonderful combination. As you read these lines, I shall be there.

Canvas pinkfeet, 27 October 1983

Shooting is about more than simply pulling the trigger as a brief glance at sporting canvases on the walls of John's home in Bottisham would confirm. In this Country Gun column from 1983, he explores the emotional response to sporting art and objects.

My circumstances prevent me becoming an art collector in the Paul Getty class, but I know what I like. Some art lovers go for the Boots Gallery best-sellers such as the green Burmese woman, the white stallions galloping through the spindrift or the pair of swans under the hawthorn blossom. To each his own, say I, and thank heavens we don't all like the same things. The question of what does or does not constitute good taste remains unsolved and ever-changing, in spite of centuries of acrimonious dispute. The shooting man tends to be attracted by pictures of his sport, the capturing on canvas of scenes and events familiar to him. Just to look at one recalls a happy or exciting time, but there is a hint of voyeurism about it since he can see wigeon flighting to a frozen bog without himself feeling cold, ambush the pinks on the merse from the comfort of his own fireside.

The picture galleries at the Game Fair are usually crowded, but picture buying is an expensive business so most of us have to settle for envious gazing. Perhaps it is as well that we are not all millionaires. since I could live happily with any of the pictures on the Tryon Gallery stand and would cheerfully buy the lot, only to find I had run out of hanging space. A real wrench comes when you fall in love with a picture and must have it. The price is far beyond what you would expect to pay, even for a green Burmese woman, so eventually you tear yourself away and suffer a few sleepless nights until the longing passes.

A shooter looks at a picture with a critical eye: the thing has to be right, down to the last detail. The impressionist or surrealist painting is not for him. If he finds himself reflecting that a pheasant could never fly in that way, or that wigeon would not be using that field in those conditions, or that a shooter would not hold his gun in that way, he shies away from the picture. Were he to buy it and look at it every day, what started as a small criticism would grow until it dominated and spoiled the whole picture. So you tend to find that the best shooting pictures are painted by artists who shoot. The Derick Bown painting of a partridge drive makes the point. Who but a shooting man would expect a straggler from a fleeing covey to be trailing a leg? I look at it and surmise when and where the bird might fall, where a picker-up ought to have been placed and what the chances are of a clean retrieve. As with much art, a great deal of its meaning lies beyond the paint and canvas and needs a spark of imagination to set it free.

Non-shooting visitors to my house look briefly at my Peter Scott (print), my Derick Bown, my Will Garfit and others. 'Ah, ducks in flight', they say, stifling a yawn. Such pictures can fall into the category of kitsch for those who see only a lurid sunset and a skein of fowl – a picture obviously painted for its striking effect. Those for whom such scenes are familiar, who can smell the mud and feel the keen wind, who hear the clamouring skeins and experience a twinge of anxiety that a shot might be 'on', look at my pictures with a more knowing eye.

Paul Getty or not, I fell under the spell of two super pictures by a young fowler/artist, Julian Novorol from Norfolk. I saw them on the Peter Keyser Gallery stand at the Scottish Game Fair, one a puntgunning scene, the other of pinkfooted geese coming in to a frosty potato field. Both caught the breath with their uncanny sense of what wildfowl and fowling are all about. I could afford neither, but if I could, which one would I choose? I strolled about brooding, in mental turmoil, and returned later in the day for another gloat. The puntgunning picture had gone! At least one decision had been made for me, but I was doomed, and slowly, inexorably I realised that the pinkfooted geese had to be mine whether I could afford them or no.

One day Securicor arrived with a stout parcel. With a feverish hand I tore off the cover and there it was – mine at last! I called down the memsahib and prepared myself for her delighted reactions: she took one look at it and crisply said, 'Very nice, but it clashes with the curtains'. Well, I ask you! Isn't that just like a woman! A casual guest dropped in the following evening. Just by chance I mentioned my new picture; just by chance it hung nearby. I indicated it with a nonchalant wave, as though buying oil paintings were an everyday event. My friend adjusted his spectacles and peered at it closely. 'Ah ducks,' was all he said. I led him quietly away, back to his drink. Any further comment on either side would have been superfluous.

Those who know see the things I see, but I did not buy my pinkfoot painting for them. I bought it for me. Every time I look at it I feel uplifted and instantly reminded of happy times and wonderful sights. Flushed with this purchase, my eye was next captured by a limited print run by the BASC to celebrate (guess what) its 75th anniversary. It is a work from the brush of that superb shooting artist, Rodger McPhail, a pot pourri of shooting scenes called 'Shooting Impressions'. The print was advertised in the current BASC quarterly magazine, and again the terrible compulsion came over me. My cheque was in the post with the ink still wet.

Now I shall have to be careful and stay well away from art galleries, auctions and catalogues. The thing could turn out to be habit forming; I am running out of walls, and constantly changing the curtains at today's prices in order to match the pictures would make even Paul Getty think twice.

The shooting element and jazz element in my life I try to keep strictly separate. Playing a trumpet in a New Orleans jazz band once a week puts me in contact with those who cannot tell a flatcoat from a Fenn or a pheasant from a fallow. I like it that way, for it makes a refreshing change from endless conversations about hard mouth, pheasant rearing, wonderful dogs and the doings of stoats. By the same token, I know no shooting man who can whistle, far less sing, 'You been a good ole waggon, honey, but you done broke down', a glaring gap in their cultural make-up for which I can blame a slack upbringing and neglected education.

Just occasionally there comes a culture warp, a face in the crowd which ought not to be there. Sudden panic and déja-vu: am I playing in the band or addressing the wildfowling club? One night, during the interval between sets I was buttonholed by Pat Henderson, one of our faithful followers. "You're a shooting man, I hear", he said. Was he about to ask advice about his gun or tell me about his dog? My heart sank, but all was well, for his shooting life-story included founder membership of the Patrington WA, an involvement in the Protection of Birds Act and a gunning life spent in the heart of Duncan country. Uncanny how that man crops up so regularly. We both bemoaned the oil slick which now threatened that very marsh, but at the time of our conversation, the geese and wigeon had still to arrive, so they might be spared.

Finally, and to my delight, he fumbled in his pocket and produced an old WAGBI badge, one of the very first, inscribed simply, 'Wildfowlers Association', with the crudely-fashioned flying goose on the red background. "That was pinned on my coat by an old chap called Stanley Duncan who founded it. Have you heard of him? I would like you to have it for the pleasure I have had from listening to the band."

His generosity may have exceeded his musical taste, but I now have another treasure over which to gloat.

Fife Safari, 3 February 1983

This feature from Shooting Times in 1983 is a perfect example of the manner in which John could take his readers along for the ride on shooting expeditions – in this instance, even a modest bag was well worth the journey.

"It's more of a removal van ye'd' be wanting," said the coach driver as he loaded my kit into his boot. I took his point; guncase, rucksack full of oilskins and boots, canvas sack with enough Alphamax cartridges to start a war, holdall with changes of clothes and other necessaries – all that for just four days in the Kingdom of Fife in pursuit of the grey geese.

Cambridge coach station at 10.30 on a wet and windy Sunday night was not the most cheering spot from which to start a journey full of such hope, and a gruff Scottish driver abusing my baggage was no British Airways hostess when it came to charm, but he certainly knew how to drive. We thundered up the motorway through swirling rain, which turned into sleet as we passed Scotch Corner. The darkened coach resembled the aftermath of an explosion with bodies lying in contorted attitudes, trying to doze as best they could while we roared through the night. I was making a mental note of what I had forgotten: binoculars, alarm clock, and hide netting had occurred to me before we had reached Stamford, but I could not have given that poor driver any more bags to carry.

Edinburgh Coach Station in a pre-dawn Monday blizzard was no more heart-warming than Cambridge had been nine hours earlier, but my depression was instantly dispelled by the towering figure of Allan Graham, one hand clutching a striped golfing umbrella, the other stretched out in welcome, his beaming smile making the raw air seem less chilly. We caught up on the gossip over one of Clare's famous breakfasts while gradually I came to terms with my coach-lag which told me it ought really to have been supper time. I was as hungry for news of geese as for bacon and eggs and heard that several birds were working the local potato land, much of it flooded after the wet weather, while the tops of the hills were white with the first snows.

That day was spent snoozing in the chair. In the evening Ian Strathearn, landlord of The Lomond Country Inn and a noted host of visiting fowlers, gave us a 'fix' on one likely field and, dark though it was, we went out to reconnoitre the ground for the morning. A swollen burn rushed greyly under the bridge; black and muddy fields stretched away into the dark; the stars blinked until the hard edge of the mountain range blacked them out. The rush of water was not loud enough to drown a babble of pinkfoot talk which floated down to us on a wind which cut us to the goose pimples. With chattering teeth, we hurried back to the warm car, sure that in the morning we would at least be in with a chance.

There were no lie-ins. Allan, his son Guy and I were gulping tea and cornflakes well before dawn and we were soon standing on the edge of the field from which distant goose music still drifted. What should we do, walk the birds off the field and let them return, or leave them to attract new arrivals? We decided to leave them and, as quietly as we could, we set out a large squad of shell goose decoys within range of the rough grass of the burn bank which represented the only available cover. Not only are these decoys of proven attractiveness, but no less than 30, plus pegs, can be carried in an ordinary shooting bag and with geese, as with other decoys, the more you have, the better.

Despite our stealth, we were still setting up our 'picture' when there was a roar of wings and a muddy thumbprint on the oil painting of the sky showed where a large skein had lifted. We distributed ourselves at the foot of the dilapidated sheep fence with its fringe of dead grass which seems to have surrounded every good goose field I can remember. Mallard and wigeon were also enjoying the potato feast, for quacks and whistles punctuated the goose gabble and 'wink wink' which came from the geese still undisturbed down the far end. Several large skeins came over from the loch, all of them pinks, forming and reforming in chevrons and wedges, a bead curtain rising and falling across the grey dawn. We pressed ourselves into the dead grass, peeping upwards and sideways to watch them pass.

Then a smaller group, 30 strong, swung round from behind, much lower. They saw the decoys and planed round into the wind. We gave them a short burst of calling, but must have shown a white face, as, for no apparent reason, they began to beat their wings again and flew on over the field. A pricked or widowed greylag was struggling to keep up with the pinks: he was honking plaintively and thought about joining the decoys but decided to play for safety and continued to follow his stronger companions.

Skeins, some of them numbering hundreds of geese, filled the sky for about an hour, one moment starkly clear against the snowy mountainside, the next a smudgy patch against the pink of the dawn. Their music was constantly in our ears and I lay there entranced. A warning whistle from Allan made me screw round my head to see a score of geese with wings set coming to the decoys. They were decidedly shootable and when they were directly overhead, I rose to one knee and fired two careful shots, threes in the first barrel, ones in the second. They might just as well have been grains of rice for I was well behind. Geese, even planing on set wings, are deceptively fast, those great wings and bodies mesmerising the eye and tempting the shooter to 'poke' at them. My two companions fired at a similar party a little later but sadly they fared no better than I had done. At the shots, the birds burst out clamouring, threshed their wings to gain height and swung away downwind towards the water.

By now the sun was up and, caught in its rays, the decoys looked even more attractive, rocking gently on their pegs. Several parties of geese came from the far side of the field to have a look at them, but none offered a fair chance. A good flight of pigeon began to build up, coming from the belt of firs to settle on the stubble beyond the burn. One should not fire at duck, let alone pigeon on a goose flight, but they made a tantalising sight as, 15 yards up, they flopped over our hides.

It seemed that the geese had finished with us. It was already 10am and Allan suggested that we began a decoy collecting session. Obediently I was just setting out when Guy hissed, "Geese, behind you!" A new flight line had begun, this time the birds were passing behind us to land on a large meadow on the far side of the pigeons' pine trees. Someone suggested we gave it another 10 minutes, but it was only a short burst of activity and I stood up again only to drop like a stone as I saw a skein of about 50 birds coming straight in from the loch; 49 of them swung away just when they were coming into range, but the 50th inexplicably held his course.

Ignoring wings and body, I tried to imagine his head as a driven partridge, swung and fired one shot. There was a pause of half a heartbeat and I heard the pellets strike *phruttt* like a handful of dried peas flung at an umbrella. One wing went up, the great shape collapsed and was falling, falling to thump down onto the field with complete and exhilarating finality. In a second I had it swinging by the paddles, a gander of well above average size and enough years of wisdom to have made a mystery of his fatal moment of carelessness. It was the sort of bird, as Allan Allison remarked later, to hang for a fortnight and then give away.

My companions, true sportsmen both, raised a cheer and their hats at my good fortune: such happenings are 90% luck at the best of times.

Good to be back, 5 September 1991

Back on the grouse moor, for the start of another season, John and his companions work hard for their sport. The opening day in amongst the heather offers the chance to christen the season and exercise some neglected muscles.

Apart from ourselves, the only animated presence seemed to be the wind. Like a great weight it leaned firmly but gently against me, flicking my coat collar into my eye before it hissed through the stiff stems of the cotton grass. Billowing clouds rolled overhead, chasing off the little patches of blue, hardly big enough to mend a Dutchman's trousers, but successive swathes of light and shade swam across the grey-green flank of the valley below.

A mysterious bird accompanied our march, flying from tussock to tussock way beyond number one Gun. It wailed eerily and rhythmically like the squeaking of a rusty pub sign, on and on for half an hour, like a bird of ill omen following a doomed army to its final battle, a suitably chilling sound for a wild and lonely place. I had it down tentatively for a merlin, but Richard, our towering Orcadian guest, put me right. "Golden plover", he remarked succinctly. "They often do that when they have chicks about." We were to see merlins later, a pair swinging round in harmony, passing the remains of a pipit one to another, as is their charming custom.

My legs held up well, thanks to the strict training, but along with my fellow sportsmen, my head was a little delicate due to the previous night's dose of single malt, which had obviously 'gone off' in the hot weather.

The first grouse had yet to fall – a symbolic event which we celebrate each year with a modest sweepstake and much rejoicing. Who would it be? The first grouse and the first shot are by no means synonymous, so the matter was wide open. We glanced up and down; who was in the best place? Where did the heather lie most thick and promising?

In the end it was Roy, down in the less likely ground at the bottom, a single bird going back, a knock of a shot and down it went, squirt of white feather trickling over the tussocks. Hats were raised, for the season was well and truly christened, but congratulations were premature – could we find it?

First one, then two, then three dogs singly and in tandem tried for it, but could make nothing of it. We gave it a good 15 minutes before giving it the best. The first grouse had still to be retrieved so the sweep was unclaimed.

It was Tim, he of the lightning reactions and uncanny, grouse-finding skills, who finally opened the account so we could relax. Legs grew accustomed to the up and down, the broken ground, the sudden, heart-bursting slopes, unexpected gorges, wicked, green quagmires and prickly, cotton grass.

Grouse were here, there and everywhere. I missed my first but dropped the next as it slid like grease round the peat hags. It was good to feel a grouse in my hand again, an old bird, red russet and black flecked with white, feathery feet and uncut toenails, red wattles still prominent, crop stuffed with heather shoots and that smell... so distinctive. A heathery whiff, a clean moorland aroma so different from a partridge which is scented with the stubbles and red peppered thorn hedges it loves.

Up on the tops I could look back and down, almost down the farm chimneys, while a Dinky toy Land Rover crawled up the papier-mâché slope opposite and a toy man and collie went out to look at the model cows. At the drystone wall we took a breather, sprawling in the heather, comparing adventures, news from the far and often invisible end of the line filling the gaps.

"What was that long hold-up just after we started?" "We were looking for a bird which went back and seemed to fall dead, but..." "You seemed to be having a lot of shots". "Well, we found a few snipe in the wet places in those middle hags, but they take some hitting..." Inconsequential but temporarily important.

Up and going again, on easier ground now, over the plateau where the wind grew stronger. A snipe catapulted up and away and, for once, I timed my shot to match the zig rather than the zag and it fell like a pebble. I looked round triumphantly to see Robert on my left in the act of breaking his gun and looking equally triumphantly at me. Heigh ho.

Then more grouse. One moment nothing but open skies, then with a dry rustle like a calico petticoat, a covey was up, black against the early heather bloom, a rusty half-chuckle cut short, a quick mount, choose a bird, shoot, change and shoot again and sometimes it happened that a brace fell out.

It is tempting to brown when the birds appear so tightly packed, but the old rule holds good. There is a good deal of space between them, and more often than not you end up with nothing but a guilty conscience, for it is 'not done' to brown. While a purist would not shoot a bird given the risk of hitting a second, it is inevitable that if you choose one bird, sometimes another will fall by accident. Satch was good as gold with other people's birds but, when my concentration lapsed due to dealing with my own, he was... er... how shall I put it... a bit swift off the mark. All right then, he ran in. I put him on the lead for long periods during which, of course, I had no shot, took him off and walked into a fresh covey.

Lunch was at the lunch hut, but that haven of happy memory had wintered badly. The roof sagged, the uprights were rotten and leaning drunkenly. It was built during the golden era when a four-course lunch was brought up on ponies rather than the cheese sarnie, tin of Longlife and an apple carried in a shoulder bag which served us now, but it has been a powerful icon for us for 15 years. Another northern winter should see the end of it.

Then it was into the good heather, until at last we rounded the mighty shoulder of the hill and tramped on until the cars appeared way down below twinkling in the sun, but it was still a long way to go. Finally, with feet which were beginning to remind us that we had demanded more of them than for 12 months past, we were back.

The first two days put in the larder 36 brace but, as usual, very much more than this. The company, the place, the rare privilege of having the opportunity to walk there and chase the finest of all gamebirds made for priceless shooting days to recall long after the legs refuse to make that first ascent and we are left only with memories. My bird of ill-omen, be it merlin or plover, had, after all, proved a false prophet of doom.

African Steam, 27 December 2001

Of all the sporting trips John undertook in his life, one of the most memorable and luxurious was the trip to South Africa he made in 2001 with his wife Angela to experience a gameshooting safari by rail – proof that life as a Shooting Times columnist could, occasionally, be back-breaking work.

How many beaters might you reasonably expect on a driven game shoot? Ten? Maybe 20? Somewhere between the two is the norm, so to stand facing the cover while 130 of them came tapping forward was a new experience. Add to that the fact that they were all Matabele men, women and children, and you will understand that it was a mind-blowing experience.

A distant double gunshot signalled the start of the drive, at which there burst out a subdued but sinister ululation from massed throats, combined with the tapping together of two flat pieces of wood. No two pairs sounded the same note, so the combination of rippling music, of tapping and strange cries, was deeply stirring.

On a 1,000-yard front, they came through the veldt, bare legs impervious to thorns, acacia with vicious spikes, snakes and stinging insects. As on a pheasant drive in England, the unshootable stuff showed first. At home, it would be woodpigeons, the odd fox and a roe deer. Here, a sounder of warthogs dashed stiff-tailed, close enough to touch; impala sprang by on elastic legs, followed by springbok, monkeys and wild pigs, one of which demolished the reed hide of my neighbour, seconds after he made a desperate leap to safety.

On the open grassland outside the drive, a herd of tessebe antelope, closely followed by an acre of wildebeest and a mixed lot of impala and ostriches, had trotted across as a curtain-raiser. A greater kudu bull, as big as a horse with spiralling horns, thundered through the scrub. Strange birds, crying harshly and painted with all the colours of the rainbow, wafted over, as well as hawks, hornbills, giant storks and parrots.

There were no worries about 'proper' birds coming, for they were there in numbers – all wild, all sporting and all exciting. Often, the helmeted guineafowl were the curtain-raiser. There came an anxious clucking from somewhere in front. It was hard to tell from where. Like corncrakes, the birds are great throwers of their voices. Without warning and in complete silence, a great cloud of them rose well in front and came sailing past, gaining height, each flying at a slightly different angle from its neighbour. It was the classic case of flock shooting – pick your birds and stay calm. Start chasing shadows, change birds, poke and stop the swing and you make them more difficult than they are. Get it right, and two tumble down to crash through the scrub and lie still.

My team of two cheetah-swift and eagle-eyed bird boys scurried off, and in ten seconds, had both birds at my feet. This was the first of several waves, umbrella black in the blue sky. Sometimes, an odd one would sneak out at the side calling for a nippy snap shot though the thorns.

Throughout the drive, the secondary theme was francolin, usually Swainson's, with the odd Natal and crested thrown in for variety. The Swainson's is a large streaky partridge with red wattles, and the old cocks have long, sharp spurs. They fly straight, like redlegs, often curling at the last minute, sometimes flying low and unshootable, but usually well above the tree line.

The beaters drew near at last, the odd flash of brightly-coloured clothes through the scrub, a fluttering red flag and that nerve-tingling chanting coming ever closer. Then it was over. The last francolin hung on until the final second before skimming away to safety. A tiny monkey crouched in a bush in front of me pretending to be invisible.

It was a long, dusty trudge back to the vehicles, and then a sharpish 10 minutes on a tiered safari wagon to the next drive and more of the same. At the end of the day, the bag of about 200 birds was laid out, and the great army of shoot helpers gathered behind it, sitting and squatting in dead silence. There followed one of the most moving experiences of my shooting life. They made speeches and sang for us – the song of the guineafowl and a haunting anthem about the ephemeral nature of human life. Some of them would be dead before the year ended, victims of the scourge of Aids.

This singing, as the red-ball sun sank behind the thorns, in air as clear and sweet as champagne, was both moving and stirring. First, the strong female lead voice, the girls' chorus joining in. Then the deep thunder of the male backing in this wild land of iron-tough people brought genuine tears to my eyes, and glancing round at my fellow sportsmen, I could see that I was not alone. These people had so little and yet were so happy. To think that back home, where suburbanites were washing cars, mowing lawns and whinging about everything, the poorest of them was a multimillionaire compared with these folk, and yet still they were not content.

Each of the Matabele would have a guineafowl in the family pot that night, and after the issue of an orange each and a pittance of a wage, they waved us off to climb thoughtfully into our plane and depart. Before leaving, they begged for a fly past, so we banked sharply at the end of the runway and swooped low over the crowd. There was a forest of waving hands that vanished in a dense cloud of red dust, and then they were gone from our lives forever.

The expression 'trip of a lifetime' has been outworn, but this one came pretty close. We travelled on the most luxurious steam train in the world, beautifully restored Victorian carriages converted into sumptuous bed-sits with a viewing car at one end and a five-star restaurant at the other. Pink champagne flowed as we watched herds of big game from the picture windows. Each night, we pulled into a siding, and next morning, we'd fly from a small airfield to this or that vast farm for a day of shooting.

Standing to attention stood a row bird boys in neat uniforms, each wearing a badge which showed the name of his own particular shooter. Rovos Rail is rightly proud of its magnificent steam trains, and ours was to take us through Zimbabwe, Botswana and South Africa, while we flew much further afield from our travelling hotel. Such trips involve a huge amount of hard work and precise organisation, and it was a marvel to see how neatly everything fell into place, with minibuses, small planes and waiting shooting hosts. There was never a slip.

Peter Johnson, who runs these trips, has applied the principles of habitat and wild-game management to the lonely miles of the veldt. He has worked hard with his hosts to make them think about providing water, keeping the place quiet, ending poaching, judicious planting of food crops and the management of their farms to the benefit of birds. It is a tribute to his success that his wild-bird shoots have become a treat for connoisseurs. Like any wild-bird enterprise, there is much to go wrong, for breeding seasons are as uncertain there as here, and there are many predators. It was strange to find Game Conservancy Trust principles being employed so effectively in a far and savage land.

Our day with the Narnaqua sand grouse was one of many that blur into a mountain range of sporting peaks. It was a long flight and a long drive down wide, empty roads, past stately ostriches and buck in the fields. We were in the Kalahari Desert, where water is gold. At last we arrived at the Sidi Varrani ranch, pulling up in a cloud of choking dust. Three Boer farmers were there to greet us. These were hard men making a living in a hard land. We were deployed in dugout butts in the dry scrub, me with my bird boy, Renard, crouching behind. He knew not a word of English, but when something went wrong, he revealed a line of obscene profanities which would have made a sailor blush. His education had not been entirely neglected.

For half an hour, nothing happened, save that the sun gonged down from a clear blue sky, a black eagle soared and flies buzzed around my head. Then there came a strange trilling call, part whistle part coo. Their nickname is Kelkiwyn, which mimics the cry, and the first flocks of Namaqua sand grouse zipped past. I had not seen them before and they reminded me of golden plover in their tight-knit packs and straight purposeful flight. These were not going to be easy, and a spatter of shots from behind made me look round. No bird appeared to fall. None of them was slow or close, they flew fast and took some hitting. In the end, I got going and one or two started to tumble. They could carry shot amazingly and have a skin that no human fingers can tear. The old rules of good swing and smooth squeeze worked the oracle. The birds began to pile up, small in the hand, plump breasted with beautiful eyed plumage and sharp, pointed tails.

The flight lasted two-and-a-half hours with the birds coming to a tiny waterhole created by our hosts. They were not feeding young from their breast pouches, and nor was this the only water in the area. They simply changed direction and went to the next farm. Consciences were clear, for I have heard of sand grouse being shot off water holes when they were desperate to feed chicks, and I, for one, would not be happy about that.

Renard had made a neat heap of our 36 birds. The total bag for eight Guns was just short of 100, but we had seen many thousands of sand grouse that morning, all put there by thoughtful management, making a sporting occasion out of nothing. A huge breakfast appeared by the acacia tree, and the boys opened a score of sand grouse and threw them on the grill over a thornwood fire. Washed down by fine South African red, they tasted delicious. Our little plane took off and, in two hours, we were back at our mobile home, dusty and dishevelled, but greeted by our cool and delightful hostesses in their pretty frocks.

The sand grouse, francolin and guinea fowl were the main themes of the week, but on one afternoon, for variety, we ambushed the little doves flying out to roost from a maize field the size of Rutland. Here again, I had a well-made butt, with a log breastwork and palisade, and two likely lads to retrieve, and the flight began straight away.

The birds are very small, and zip past exactly like driven grouse, flaring slightly when they see the raised human face. The sun made barrels uncomfortably hot before a shot was fired, and I found I had to let them cool down a bit during the action. Adrian Lemmon, who looks after my guns, would have cross words if he found I had shot poor old Watson off the face for a third time. The doves clattered down into the dry stalks, the bird boys dashed here and there. A Swainson's francolin pitched in front, and leaving the hide, I walked it up, flushed it and knocked it down. The sun sank rapidly and my face was glowing uncomfortably when the truck came to collect us.

The boys had counted 71 doves to my tally for the expenditure of 140 cartridges, so I knew I would have worse days. These were wonderfully sporting birds, arrow swift and direct in flight. But being very small, they were usually closer to you than they seemed. At last light, great skeins of Egyptian geese and duck flighted out to the far side of the field. A small herd of zebra dashed away from the roadside, and our last sunset in Africa turned the sky blood red, then deep purple.

It had been a week of pure magic, of friendly local people, great companionship, luxury on the train and sporting shooting to die for. It was 24 hours from Bulawayo airport to Bottisham, irksome slog, but the journey was sustained by rich and varied memories.

I have to say there have been worse starts to a shooting season. Africa has set its hooks in me, and one day, I'll go back.

A sportsman's privilege, 16 March 2006

Part of the joy of shooting is the access it gives to the spectacular landscapes that make up our countryside. Here, in a Country Gun column from 2006, John reflects on the variety one season gave him.

Wise men say that shooting is about nice places and nice people. No arguments there, and looking back on the past season, apart from meeting a great many pleasant people, a good few special corners of our lovely land felt the imprint of Country Gun's wellies. One in particular was Audley End, in Essex. As I stood on a long grassy slope facing a pretty wood, I gazed down the hill, across the road to the lake speckled by duck behind it and, reflected in the water, the Palladian dream of that magnificent mansion. Staring, I was so enraptured at the view that I did not notice the first three birds fly over. For a dreamy moment I pretended to be the landowner shooting his own pheasants and having but to turn his head to see his home, one of the finest houses in England.

Another was on the Ladykirk estate, in Scotland where they show some remarkable pheasants brilliantly presented by young keeper Ian Scoby. One drive was on the banks of the Tweed, up which the silver bars of the first spring salmon were battling. The river is the Border, so a high bird might be shot in Scotland and land in England, as several were. The pickers-up were ferried with their dogs across the river in the salmon fishing cobles, and the boatmen held station in mid-river, ready to gather with landing nets birds that fell in the water. It was, as my American friends say, 'kinda neat' to shoot within 30 yards of the spot where, back in September, I landed two large salmon. To make it spookier, I fluked down a woodcock as it whizzed round the hill. At the same moment, out of my sight in the trees and two places from me, number one son David also fired at a woodcock and dropped it within five yards of mine. We each sent the picker-up for one woodcock and he returned with two. Does that count for a family right-and-left?

Back down south and again I waited at a peg and stared around. Nothing spectacular here, just another corner of old England with a thousand just like it. There was a faint haze of wood smoke from cottage fires and rearing high above the red roofs, a church steeple. Round the village was a patchwork of arable land, grass, woods, hedges, fat cattle and barns built when the Armada was sent packing. As I watched, a small herd of fallow and then a hare trotted between the village and me. The scene, unchanged for centuries, made names such as Al Qaeda and troubles in Iraq seem on another planet. Who could think of disrupting such an ancient, beloved, safe and permanent world?

Then to our own dear flat lands, more an acquired taste than some of the others, but through the familiarity of a lifetime, equally loved. No houses here, no comfortable farmsteads with drifting smoke, no cottage gardens or vegetable patches, for man is an intruder, standing 6ft below sea level on land that does not belong to him but was wrested from nature by doughty Dutch drainers long ago. The cold hand of the wind sweeps uninterrupted from the Northlands, ruffling the tawny tasselled beds of Norfolk reed, hissing through the stems like sea on shingle. A line of shock-haired willows like crouching dwarfs punctuates a horizon that almost shows the curvature of the earth. Above it, the vast dome of the heavens on a frosty morning splashed with all the colours of an artist's palette. Dykes lie sword straight and silver across earth as black as soot. A dotted line of wigeon whistles across the firmament, on creaking wings five swans fly down river. The snug corners hold little wild pheasants and woodcock, the same species, certainly, but surely not the same birds we pursue on more comfortable, higher ground.

Add to those the dangerous, wild beauty of the salt marsh, the high heather moors and the cosy brown coverts of Norfolk and no one could argue that we shooters are privileged for the wonderful places to which our sport takes us.

Sport with Family

Sharing time with friends and those you love
was central to John Humphreys' sporting life.
He often wrote about shooting on home
ground in Cambridgeshire and many
readers of **Shooting Times** were familiar
with the regular sporting tales of No. 1 and
No. 2 sons, David and Peter Humphreys,
and the exploits of the family gundogs.
All these are represented in this
section of personal tales.

Lords Ground, 22 October 1998

The 'home shoot' will be familiar to many, whether it's a village syndicate, a farm knockabout with a couple of friends or something altogether grander. Lords Ground, a few miles from John's home in Cambridgeshire was his 'home shoot' – and a winner of the Laurent Perrier Award for Wild Game Conservation. In 1998 he told the tale of a day for **Shooting Times.**

K nowing that Tim Scrivener was coming to take photographs of the shoot, I made two sartorial errors. One was to wear my 'Newmarket trainer' cloth cap, which I bought at the Game Fair and vowed would be worn only in familiar company. The second was to sport some sawn-off waders. Well, it seemed mad to waste them just because the tops were frayed and holey as the bottom halves were perfectly sound.

I suppose it speaks of my frugal wartime upbringing – all that 'waste not, want not' business, which was part of everyday life. If the invitation to Sandringham is in the post, don't worry chaps, I have better gear in the wardrobe. Proper sportsmen do not judge a shoot on whims of fashion. Our partridges are mostly wild, with a tiny rearing programme of four pens just to thicken them up. Touching wood, we claim to have had no disease, no predation in the pens and, thanks to Keith Blows' hard work, not a single loss.

You hear some bad stories. One shoot lost every reared partridge and cancelled all shooting. You hear of bags in the high hundreds where shooting has ceased to be a sport and has become hard-nosed business. All this is rumour, but the tendrils of the shooting grapevine are humming.

Have we overdone it, gone too far, become greedy and tried to exploit our wild game and wild places? They did it in the so-called 'golden era' when estate vied with estate to see which could amass the highest pile of the slain. It failed then and it will surely fail now. Small bags of sporting birds, good company, fun and laughter are what we need, and the sooner we begin to educate the corporate-day customer to that, the healthier our sport will be.

That's the sermon over – well, I am writing this on a Sunday. I can state quite baldly that yesterday on Lords Ground in the Cambridgeshire fens, we shot the amazing bag of 62, mostly partridges, which was almost double what we managed on our first day out. Every bird was remembered, talked about and analysed, though not as critically as the misses. We all enjoyed it, the sun shone and a brisk breeze helped the birds to fly.

Two years ago this shoot won the late-lamented Laurent Perrier Award for Wild Game Conservation, thanks entirely to a new farming policy and hard work by a team of working Guns. An environmentally barren agribusiness eventually became a patchwork of new woodlands, rough verges and untrimmed dykes. Washland on the Cam was left rough, willows were planted and ponds dug. Where poor wheat once grew, willows sighed in summer breezes, blackcaps nested, kingfishers darted and hen pheasants crept in the tall grass. That this had been achieved at little cost to agricultural production is a marvel, for the farm is run by Greens of Soham with ruthless efficiency. It was this double-edged sword that, we think, caught the eye of the judges. What an example to other farms and – in spite of the publicity the award received – how rarely it has been followed. The result was that bags of almost all wild birds rose from 172 to 930 in five years, with good stocks left each spring. That pinnacle was not sustained, and since then has fluctuated wildly according to the weather – the final arbiter of all wild-bird shoots. This year is a case in point. Who would have believed that after one wet June, another would follow? The habitat was well managed, with farming sensitively carried out and the vermin controlled – and yet heavy rain in the 'flaming' month virtually wiped out all the hard work. Barren pairs were common, while hen pheasants with one or two chicks in tow moped on the verges.

Such is the gamble, such the appeal and excitement of the wild-bird shoot. Disappointment is always round the corner, yet when it comes right the benefits are great. In a world of moderate reared gamebirds, ours are star performers. Who perpetuates the plain untruth that fen pheasants do not know how to fly? Birds explode from the cover. There's no need to throw a stick at them to make them rise, as they rocket up vertically looking round for the best escape route. They can go to any point on the compass, because they have no cosy feed ride or rearing wood to draw them home. I have seen them pass Guns out of range of the ground – and that is a very high pheasant indeed.

Every year the cropping pattern is different so each season is a new tactical test. Crop rotation is a challenge that keeps the adventure fresh – some drives will have never before been done that way in the 20 years we have been there.

The third drive of the morning was typical. The farm is a noted grower of daffodils, so each spring we are bathed in enough yellow for 20 Wordsworths to eulogise over. In autumn they die back, and fat-hen and other weeds so beloved of partridges grow in their place. The dry, brown fields with gentle ridges are what these birds like best. A wind was blowing down the length of four such fields and the beaters set off from the distance, their flags waving, the dry polythene whipcracks audible even that far away.

The Guns were placed according to the wind and, as usual, were invited to use their initiative. A leakage of birds from a corner would have the nearest Gun easing that way to cut them off, or the wind moving slightly to command a gap in the poplars. A peg with a card on it can be a tyrant, an anchor point which you desert at your peril. We save the time we would need to peg out and spend it on extra feeding – a shift in the wind overnight would make the exercise meaningless anyway.

We faced the wind, staring at the low horizon where clouds scurried, hearkening to the hiss of the wind in the grass and the distant 'chuk-chuk' of a redleg somewhere out in front. The beaters moved through the grazing sheep – taking care because the electric fence had already surprised several gundogs – through our best wood, but quietly so as not to disturb the pheasants, and out into the brown bulb fields. There came one shot from the far end of the line, then another. Next there was a pale flicker of wings as a good covey burst out at the corner. A doctor took a neat right-and-left, a captain of industry on his right took a singleton and a fourth bird turned back up the line where it was neatly felled by a journalist.

I was well back at the end of the line, but one redleg came buzzing back to pass me wide and curl round behind me. It was a long but safe chance, and allowing lots of lead, I fired once. The bird staggered and wobbled on to pitch far back in the tall weeds, on the side of the new farm reservoir. Head picker-up Neville Ling was already on the spot. Negotiating the dyke, he had his leash of Labradors bustling in the cover and then I saw the distant figure hold the bird aloft in triumph.

It was my only shot of the drive, but I recall it still. The hard chance, the worry lest it be lost, the shrewd placement by Neville and a good retrieve by good dogs. Who could ask more? In addition, I watched – good shooting by others, worried that they had left too large a gap in the line, enjoyed the wild scenery and was happy just to be there. To have shot a pile of flappers would not have afforded me more pleasure, but less.

After a lengthy lunch we drove one of the new woods, though being 12 years old it's not really that new. It's hard to know how to work it in a tricky wind, but the Guns crept in like Indians on the warpath and the beaters brought in a large field of sugar beet and another patch of bulbs. The wood has become a haven for plants, butterflies, warblers and small animals. Shooting has made it a retreat for wildlife.

One of our reared coveys had sheltered in it, and along with several pheasants, the birds came zipping out in small batches. Unfortunately they all flew over three Guns and did not do as we had hoped by fanning out over the line.

Our beaters are superbly led by Vinnie Jones lookalike Kevin Bailey, and we would not trade them for any in the land. Mostly they come free of charge and they are there because they want to share our fun. There may be other shoots where this is so, but I bet they are few. In fact, much of the success of Lords Ground depends on the generosity of many people – farm staff who do that bit extra, tractor drivers, cornbaggers, beaters and the Gun who invited us all to his home for bangers and mash on a winter's night. Feeders are made, footbridges over dykes constructed and the beaters' wagon painted as a labour of love.

This is what we value in our shoot. We think we have got it right and we treasure what has taken so long to build up. Those who pay for the huge bags of poor-flying birds, knocked down at so many ££s (plus VAT) a throw, and know nothing of the countryside, miss the whole point of what shooting is about. Such is not sport.

Our future is not assured. Change is in the wind and our security of tenure is uncertain. Such is the way of the world, which is full of shoots built from nothing that are then taken back in hand. Whatever the future holds, days like this will remain etched in the memory.

Black tornado, 6 February 1986

Ajax, Kenzie, Satch, Tess, China... John shared his shooting days with a long line of much-loved gundogs. It was not unknown, as in this Country Gun column from 1986, for one these minor canine celebrities to show less than complete enthusiasm for their master's voice.

Be warned: be careful before you accompany an artist in the shooting field for, should that artist happen to be a cartoonist with a wicked sense of humour, a shrewd eye and a grudge, you deserve all you get. It all started with a photograph in my new book *Learning to shoot* which shows John Paley taking delivery of a grouse from his stately flatcoat Joe. The caption, 'Do not allow your dog to retrieve another man's bird unless asked', was an attempt to cash in on a good photograph and use the caption to make a good teaching point. Joe is far too dignified and well-mannered to 'poach' another dog's bird.

How ironic, therefore, that when John and I with Joe and Kenzie in attendance spent a happy autumn day tramping the Fens, it was Kenzie who, not once, but regularly, committed the very crime against which I had warned. A black tornado, he snatched runners and dead birds alike from beneath the Roman nose of Joe, whose face registered growing surprise and distaste as might an Edwardian gentleman encountering someone wearing brown boots at a Society wedding. John subsequently sketched a cartoon marking the encounter and I cannot deny him the sweetness of revenge.

Mind you, having a quick dog is no bad thing in rough, Fen shooting. It is especially hard country for picking runners which, because of the lack of thick cover, tend to travel great distances before they find a place to 'tuck in'. My experiences picking-up in thick woodland suggested that a bird marked down in the cover may be difficult to find, but it is likely to be within yards of where it touched down. A Fen runner is not uncommonly picked a quarter of a mile from the fall and I have seen them retrieved from twice that distance.

Certainly, a 'first bounce' retriever has his uses on a walked-up day in roots thick enough to hide a running pheasant but not sufficiently dense to cause him to go to ground. All of which brings me to Kenzie, now in his sixth rumbustious year. It is a surprising thing, but the more I travel the land meeting this or that shooting group, the more people came up and ask me about him. When I had good, well-mannered dogs (yes, it has happened), nobody showed more than passing interest in them. This dog, a law unto himself, workaholic fearless to the point of foolhardiness, strong-willed and disobedient, seems to have struck a chord of sympathy. Perfect strangers approach me and ask, "How's Kenzie? He sounds very much like my old dog." A world peopled with Kenzie's might not suit everybody, but the regularity with which I hear the remark suggests a big whitewash, a gigantic cover-up, for all we seem to read about are the well-trained, drawing room-mannered gundogs which do everything so well that they give the reader an instant inferiority complex. Surely, you must be the only person in the land with a bad dog. You can fool all the people some of the time so dog owners take comfort. Just watch closely the dogs of your fellow shooters during a season and you will conclude that your own monster, for all his faults, is not that bad after all.

Kenzie and I have shared a turbulent half decade in the shooting field. On the debit side he refuses to 'sit' and does not at all care for walking to heel, two of the most basic lessons which I have drummed into him daily since he arrived as a wobbly-legged, big-footed puppy. Would you not have thought that 5,000 repetitions would have given him the idea? Still I refuse to give up. "Sit! Sit! SIIIIT!" I say, pressing down his great rump as I have been doing ineffectually for six years. He slowly and reluctantly sinks to a precarious squat, but the moment I straighten my back, he is up again and glaring around for something to ravage. A battle of the Titans follows with whacks sounding like the beating of old carpets and accompanied by about the same amount of dust, but it is impossible to chastise him.

He is a dog who believes that 100 per cent effort must be put into every minute of a shooting day. He spends his lunch hour hunting the bushes round the barn or retrieving game about to be hung in the larder. He is an oversized, craggy and muscular sort of dog but when hunting he thinks he is a little springer, bursting through brambles, quartering the steeply-angled sides of dykes, investigating every nettle stem, and emerging festooned with burrs and bell vine on the far side of thorn clumps.

He does not enter the water with the dignity of the years, or like a Victorian maiden lady in a bathing machine, but takes a flying leap from the top of the bank, like an Olympic butterfly champion, landing several feet out in an eruption of spray and pondweed. He often displays a lack of foresight and circumspection in his extravagances. At the end of the season I dropped a cock which fell dead on the far side of a thinly frozen lake to land almost under the overhang of the bank. Any dog with half a brain but less heart would have trotted round on the path, leaned over and picked the bird without getting his paws wet. Kenzie took one look, did his circus leap, crashed through the ice and ploughed a slow, determined channel across the far side, his great chest heaving as he burst the floes asunder.

He reached the bird, grabbed it, turned to retrace his path, suddenly realised how close he was to the shore and only then stepped out and galloped back via the sensible route. This enormous energy and imperviousness to pain has produced a spectacular succession of runners for the bag and once he caught a French partridge in mid-air as it flew low across a drain. He launched himself into the air like a leaping salmon and fell, with the bird in his jaws, with a hideous crash to the water eight feet below.

The self-inflicted punishment is taking its toll. He groans in his sleep and in the evening after a shooting day he can barely stagger to the hearth-rug. The recent discovery of the pink pills, one before and one after a shooting day, have made for a great easement of his rheumatics (I wonder if they work for humans) but still he has to pay for his colossal workload. He lies at my feet now, his face scarred and nose hairless after bursting through a thousand reed clumps, his ears cut, eyes scratched and sore, his cranium deeply punctured in a dozen places by blackthorns. His great carcase is bony and spare after a hard season.

His many friends will be pleased to know that he is very much alive, well, and good for many a long day yet. Fellow sufferers unite! For all their faults, we would not care to trade such dogs for the best knee-huggers in the kingdom. Whether Kenzie's master will be able to keep up with him indefinitely is another matter altogether.

Not Biting the Bullet, 30 January 1986

The notorious Labrador Kenzie was a fussy eater – not so Fen, Peter Humphreys' tawny owl, as this article from 1986 reveals. Here, home shoot from wayward hounds to a decidedly unusual quarry-specific wager in the pub.

How is it that a large, black Labrador that eats his food on the principle that the quicker you gobble it down the less chance there is of having it stolen, is able to pick out of it a single pellet of No. 7 shot? Dogs are not usually dainty eaters and Kenzie can polish off, in two minutes flat, a trough of Valumix, gravy, meat, vegetables, bread and bacon-rind mixed into a hideous potage. Included in his *plat-du-jour* will be a few hearts, boiled gizzards and scraps of skin from any gamebirds which the chef has prepared for table and sometimes, there is bound to be an odd pellet embedded in the tissue.

Like the princess and the pea, a dog's dinner proves a less than adequate hiding place for even such a small object, for check the bowl at the end and find it, as usual, polished clean and there, rolling around forlornly in the bottom will be one or sometimes more pellets of shot. Given that, like a wolf, a dog wolfs his food and does not masticate, how can he possibly sort them out and eject them? The occurrence is too regular to be coincidence.

Even a human eater who chews each mouthful the recommended number of times (it used to be 50), can have a problem picking them out for, all too often, the teeth clamp shut on a No. 3 and a searing pain strikes through an upper molar directly into the frontal lobe of the brain. Did not doctors once operate on a gamekeeper and remove from his appendix more than enough mixed shot to reload a magnum cartridge? Only by such a rare and unusual occurrence can one be made to realise how many pellets pass through the human system. It gives a new meaning to the term, 'pattern plate'.

I return to my theme; how and why does a dog manage to reject so assiduously the pellets in his food?

Shooting at a famous but miniature Cambridgeshire shoot in early January turned out to be a day full of surprises. It was a cock pheasant day, but the opening drive produced a tufted duck, four mallard, three pigeon, two Canada geese and a greylag. The final bag of about 100 head included almost everything save grouse and capercaillie.

Such a day could be a nightmare for the cartridge fanatic obsessed with matching the ammunition to the quarry; he would find himself ill-prepared with an ounce of sevens when the Canadas approached unexpectedly, change swiftly to magnum BBs, only to see them veer away and a flickering snipe pass within easy range. On this day such a shooter would have been driven to tears selecting the shot sizes he needed to do justice to such a bewildering variety of quarry.

The cocks-only policy is observed throughout the season, the object being to encourage wild hen pheasants and, with them, a healthy, indigenous stock so much preferred to reared birds. The rule is carefully observed but the prevailing direction of the winter sun can make it a matter of vexation to make a snap identification of a bird which appears as a fleeting silhouette against the brassy glare. At least one of my fellow *Shooting Times* contributors is lucky enough to shoot on this ground and his jinx is to draw a peg which has him squinting into the sun for what he feels is more than his fair share of the day. Nobody is perfect and he has earned a reputation for being what King Edward VII once termed dryly and in similar circumstances, 'a man for the ladies'.

Thus it was that when, on my day, Kenzie disgraced me (a thing he has a penchant for doing) by retrieving a lively hen pheasant from the depths of the brambles, my host was kind enough to let me off the hook by thinking on his feet almost as quickly as he shoots. With humble apologies I tendered the hen at the end of the drive but no problem, for he observed breezily, "Not to worry, old boy; probably one of Colin's runners from last week."

Sharp on opening time at The Royal Oak, a volley of shooting men and their dogs rattles through the door, the hounds running for the hearthrug, the old Fen gunners sinking onto the corduroy-polished settles along the wall. Neighbouring and rival shooting parties trickle in later, more dogs, more faces, more plus-twoed bottoms on the benches. Badinage, repartee, lies and shooting scandal zips and crackles to and fro. Conversation is overheard in fragments: "Was that head or brace, old boy?... he couldn't hit a barn door... I sent out old Ben... did you see Jim kill that cock by the firs?... the shot rattled all round me... anyone see that fox?... it looked a dead bird to me, but it must have run", and suchlike timeless observations.

Then, the silences lengthen, the talk loses its early fervour and we grow ruminative, but the lull is only temporary. The debate moves round to how much might a good cock pheasant weigh, how much a hen, a partridge, a pigeon? Nothing if not pragmatists, we settle the matter there and then, for specimens of each abound in the many town and country vehicles in the car park. The landlady brings in her kitchen scales and a modest book is opened.

Each bird is passed from hand to hand, non-shooting strangers included, hefted carefully, a judgement made and a modest wager placed. There were wildly conflicting guesses and the view expressed that the local butcher should have been debarred from entering, until some wag suggested that he was so used to adding his thumb to the weight of everything, that he was labouring under an inbuilt handicap. Not for us the new-fangled, metric weights; pounds and ounces were good enough for grandad and for Vera's scales so they were more than good enough for us. Mention a gramme in The Oak and they think you are talking about a record-player.

Our cock pheasant tipped the scale at 2lb 14oz, the hen was 2lb exactly, a chubby French partridge was 1lb 4oz, a pigeon a surprising llb 8oz, and a choice rat was llb 2oz. The latter was my own contribution, found run over on the road and bagged in order to feed Fen, No. 2 son's tawny owl. It was handed round discreetly veiled in a polythene bag, for even in The Oak, locals out to impress wives or girlfriends might not take kindly to being pressed into a rat-weighing competition.

Trouble is, what shall we do with our early evenings when the shooting season is over?

Redlegs and black faces, 1 November 1990

Some days stick in the memory not so much for the quality of the sport, but rather for the quality of the weather – in this instance, Lords Ground was more akin to the Oklahoma Dust Bowl than the fens.

"Never seen anything like it: not at this time of year, anyways up." The old timer sipped thoughtfully at his mild and bitter. Outside the pub the gale shrieked through the tatters of the last leaves of summer, slates clattered and skipped into the lane and there was no doubt that the safest place was in the four-ale bar, stockinged feet stretched luxuriantly before the log fire, surrounded by fellow sportsmen all of whom were conscious of having braved a cataclysmic and elemental day about as wild as any the old fen could show.

Out on those bare and flat wastes of which we had so recently been a part, the wind tore unhindered from the south-west. It was so strong that we staggered sometimes and hats flew off and went whirling and tumbling over the drill, providing onlookers with comic relief as owners chased after them.

The wind we could have withstood, for we are used it, but when the wind bore on its breath a billion particles of fen soil it became very trying indeed. Great black clouds of silty dust, baked powder-dry by months of sun, lifted into the air, were caught by the gale and hurled into our faces with a rasping, stinging blast, eyes were red-rimmed and sore, ears full and faces blackened in minutes. We looked like participants at the Al Jolson Fan Club annual reunion.

Looking along the fen road we could see where suddenly it vanished in black fog, cars put on their lights to pass through it while we lunatics, men of an age when we should have known better, were out in it, exposed to its worst.

At least the beaters had their backs to it. Nothing would fly into that lot, so the Guns stood propped up against the storm, eyes screwed up against the flying debris but at the same time alert and ready to shoot a partridge should one be persuaded to take wing.

Through the murk the smudged outline of a beater half appeared, his white flag a streaming pennant as he struggled to control it. It was a re-enactment of a surrender in a desert sandstorm. Gradually he took shape, coming and going as the clouds opened, closed and swirled around him. He reached the end, the whistle shrilled and he sank thankfully onto a straw bale. His face was that of a chimney sweep on a bad day, only the whites of his eyes and flashing teeth giving away his position when he moved.

At lunch we removed our hats to entertain each other with curiously two-toned features, especially those with thinning hair on whom the sudden contrast between sooty black features and pinkish white pate was quite startling.

What, you may ask, of the partridges? Enough to say that they were the best partridges a whole world of partridge shoots could produce. Never have I seen higher or faster birds, tiny specks in the howling blur of the smog. This one surely a high pigeon, but a second glance through screwed-up eyes showed it to be what it was, so tall, flying almost sideways and only just in control it hurtled over. To mount and fire was itself a minor triumph, while to bring one down was the stuff of dreams.

When a bird was hit it whirled on, a tiny black ball to drop 60 yards behind, to smack into the ground with a squirt of feathers, to bounce a further 20 yards and bounce again before coming to rest, like those bombs in the Dam Busters. For us to gather eight brace of them, all wild birds, was as good as any sackful of reared ones tamely shot in shirtsleeve weather as barely they topped the tall thorn hedge, although, mind you, the chance would be a fine thing.

Sometimes a pheasant came, not as high at the partridge by a long way, but blown ragged, curling at incredible speed, seeing the Guns at the last minute and rocketing up with the wind in his tail. Not many of those were shot either.

There came a hoarse cry from overhead and I looked up to see a heron battling into the wind. His heart was set on going that way – he wanted to go there so much, more than anything else in the world. For a living minute he flapped mightily to stay in the same place. Then – and you could almost hear him thinking it – he reflected that he would drop back a few yards for a breather and try again.

Back he slid, those canopy wings flailing frantically and then once more he faced the front, only to indulge in another titanic struggle, but with no more success than he had last time. Once more he dropped back and again he tried, but equally fruitlessly, to head for whatever heron paradise he had set his heart on.

In the end he gave up and with a harsh 'krank' of frustration he turned and whirled away in the general direction of Ely. Again one could almost hear him thinking, 'Well, I didn't really want to go that way anyway, dammit.' Here was a heron with none of the blood of Robert the Bruce's spider.

So now it was all over. The head beater and his team were all there for love (shame on those who talk about money in the same breath as beating) and they looked about all in. "Just one more?" they said, and just one more it was, for the human frame can take only so much.

The washbasins at The Red Lion were clogged with our grime but we got most of it off and sat there at our ease while outside the storm raged unabated. Faces glowed, grime still lurked behind many an ear, and eyes wept black tears, but at least we were out of it, job done, challenge offered and met with valour.

The old timer was absolutely right: this was the place to be. No risk of getting blown away or covered in dust like the guns, cameras and lunches, all impregnated with the black fen, which would never be the same again.

I have never known a storm yet which did not look all the better from the cosy fireside of an old village pub.

A grand finale, 2 February 2006

Six Mile Bottom, just a stone's throw from John's home at Bottisham, is a name celebrated by gameshooters. In 2006, the future of the estate's shoot was uncertain – so John and his 'Dad's Army' of Guns were adamant that they were going to enjoy every last minute of their day's sport.

'**D**ad's Army' girded its loins, adjusted its surgical appliances, inserted hearing aids, took its pills and potions and, weighed down by cartridges, lurched up to Six Mile Bottom for some fun. It was like a Saga holiday, with keeper and shoot manager Richard Clarke as the rep keeping us all in order. This was more than just our special annual day, for it was the last season that famous shoot would be operating in the old way. For more than a century, Six Mile Bottom (6MB) has been a byword for fine sport, but nothing is forever and it was a wise man who said the only way to guarantee your shooting was to buy it. Got £10million anyone?

No gloom today though, except in the weather, which was freezing fog and silky calm. No worries for 'Dad's Army', as they like to see birds they can hit, but Richard and his beaters were whistling for some wind. As it happened it came after lunch and then the birds were as sharp as you could wish. So well organised are things at 6MB that you drive what seems like miles in the luxurious Guns' wagon, clamber out and the lines of beaters are there already, with red flags bearing down on the cover. After the drive, off we go again, seemingly across half of Suffolk, stop and lo and behold, there are the same beaters converging on a new place. There is no hanging about. Some wag suggested that the wagon just drove back and forth along the same lane, but there can be no foundation for such a malicious rumour – can there?

I was back Gun, a supernumerary, but no worries there. Better back Gun in the middle than proper Gun stuck miles out on an end, sez I. No shortage of birds wherever you stood, for they shovelled over. We ended the day with about 250 wonderful pheasants and redlegs.

The thing about 6MB is the easy feel to it all. No one gets tense, beaters are quiet and efficient, the food turns up piping hot in a remote spot, and our famous Newmarket sausages dipped in mustard and washed down with sloe gin never tasted better. As for high birds, you shoot what you like and what is within your compass and nobody passes comment. The hot Shots who fancy themselves wait for the higher ones, those of more moderate skill select those that suit them. Nobody likes being humiliated by too difficult birds. The 'I'm a high bird man' snobbery is really rather sad and loses sight of what we are there for, which is to have fun.

The day drew to an end as the fog closed round us like a shroud. Over tea in the gunroom, Richard showed us a photograph of King George V in a shooting party in the first decade of the 20th century, standing where we had stood. We smiled more than they did; they seemed to take the whole thing very seriously. Nor would they have done as we did and returned to Humphreys' Towers to a feast of wild pheasant stew and my home-grown vegetables prepared by the *memsahib*, while in the grate ash logs flared red and orange, dogs snoozed and curtains were drawn against the cold night air. As for Richard, he tells me his ambition is to become a licensed victualler and landlord of a country pub. He hopes to maintain his shooting in the area. His hostelry [The Green Max, in Six Mile Bottom] will serve traditional meat and fish, English-style, and his dream features old ale and roaring fires. I hope shooting folk passing by as well as locals will support the venture in return for all that Richard has given to the shooting world.

Whether 'Dad's Army' will stagger out again with Richard next Christmas is in the hands of the gods. We can but hope…

A timeless sport, 15 March 2007

With a peregrine soaring overhead, the South East Falconry Group wait in eager anticipation for an end-of-season pheasant to make a break for it in their annual trip to Lords Ground.

It was a scene frozen in time. Alone in the middle of a bleak fen field, the falconer stood statue still, a man carved from anthracite, his head thrown back, he stared at the heavens like some ancient sun worshipper. You could almost see the curvature of the earth on that cold, bright day with a breeze and snowdrops drifting in the hedge bottom. A thousand feet above his head, a black crossbow shape circled lazily, sometimes almost hovering, a peregrine 'waiting on' they call it, ready for the moment of the stoop, the assassin hurtling earthwards at a hundred miles an hour to sound the crack of doom for some unlucky quarry. I wondered what view the falcon had of us in her lofty position, tow'ring in her pride of place, as Shakespeare said. She would see upturned white faces, the chessboard of black fields with strips of thin covercrops, she could see the serpentine river winding towards the sea, flocks of gulls, pigeon, rooks and peewits. From her vantage point she would see the gaggle of Canadas and swans feeding on a corn drill in the next village. She could see the dog, rock still on point below and far away the pointing finger of the great tower of Ely cathedral.

Man, bird, dog and pheasant watched each other warily – who would be the first to crack? The pheasant was the one for which to feel sorry. The falcon came round again, a pinprick in the vault of the sky, almost stalling when she reached perfect pitch. The spell broke, the man moved, the dog started and the pheasant burst from cover as ready as it would ever be to face what was coming. It made height and set off like a good'un towards the distant smudge of the covercrop. But there was a swifter bird on the wing and the falcon tipped on to one side, made itself thin as a scalpel blade and sliced down the sky at breathtaking speed. This was what it was all about, this was what we had come to see. The falcon hit the pheasant with the sound of a tennis racket striking a cabin trunk and for a second bound on, but it was a strong, end-of-season bird. The deadly talons missed the small of the back by an inch and instead gripped the thick pad on the rump, failed to make purchase, a cloud of feathers flew out and drifted to snag on the willow twigs. The pheasant gave a crow of triumph and dived into cover, falcon in hot and fruitless pursuit a yard behind its tail.

So much for a taste of our day with the South East Falconry Group on our little shoot, an event which has marked the dying of the season for almost 20 years. We had a team of 15 or so of the most beautiful peregrines with their owners, assorted dogs and hangers-on and, as is our way, meandered aimlessly round the farm from this point to that, finding less game than usual and suffering more than our share of fly-offs, where the falcon departs into the wild blue yonder and calls for a leg-numbing walk by its owner to retrieve it. I would not wish to open a poultry shop on the proceeds of our days, but that is not the point. As Kenzie Thorpe used to say, 'It's the sport, man, it's the sport.'

Club chairman and old pal Gary Biddis was field captain, sporting what looked like a duelling scar on his lower lip where his bird had grabbed him playfully with one of its front talons. Lucky for him it was not the murderous hind toe and not in his eye. It seems to be a sport for the patient, the stoical and the philosophical. To see these paragons in the flesh and in display mode you need only turn up at the Fenland Country Fair on August Bank Holiday Sunday and Monday at Stow-cum-Quy near Cambridge.

Pottering for England, Country Life, *16 December 2009*

The Boxing Day shoot encapsulates all that is good about gameshooting, as this piece from Country Life *illustrates. It is a day when nostalgia, tradition, self-indulgence and seasonal indigestion combine to bring everyone closer together.*

C atch a hard-bitten shoot captain after his fourth sloe gin, and he will confess that one of his favourite days is what is variously termed the 'boys' day', 'the family day', 'the knockabout', or even in one case, 'the gang bang'. This is when those we love the most sport together. Where lack of a shotgun or knowledge of the sport is no bar to participation. Camp beds are wrestled into submission, viands and cases of wine broken out and the kitchen staff go into meltdown planning menus. Room for visiting dogs must be found, incoming shotguns stored securely, and boots, coats and cartridge bags piled in what you call your gunroom.

Should your loved ones voice concern about the idiosyncrasies of Uncle Henry, remind them of the age of the Big Shots. Visiting royalty arrived with 50 hangers-on, keepers, loaders, valets, dog men, mistresses, assorted offspring and chums, much as a boxing champion travels with an entourage of admiring sycophants. Once the host has found room for this army, he strips his cellar of its finest wines, Napoleon brandies, Havana cigars and provides patrician feasts. For the following week, his noble guests decimate the wildlife on his estate, drink him dry and leave him a poorer and certainly a wiser man. Two legendary Victorian Shots were beggared by providing shooting hospitality and found obscure graves overseas.

The family day falls ideally on Boxing Day, when country folk have gone a'sporting since William Rufus notched arrow to bow. It is a private day, and although the host reminds everyone how relaxed it will be, how unstructured and how irrelevant the bag, beneath a jovial exterior, he's a mass of anxieties. The simple act of organising transport from home to shoot is fraught, for no non-shooter cares to expose his upholstery to muddy dogs. In the field, non-combatants are there to share the occasion, but must be kept safe and left in no doubt that they must stay in-line… literally. This comes hard to Uncle Joe, bossy managing director of the cement works, not used to being shouted at to 'keep up' by an eight year old. Nothing takes the edge off Christmas like getting the family peppered.

But tush, I protest too much, for it's a lovely day. All rules, save those of safety, may be relaxed, the size of the bag is immaterial, no pressure, and the party wallows in a Pickwickian haze of nostalgia and tradition. Family and friends have shot the home patch on Boxing Day since Jethro Tull was tinkering.

Our family outing takes place on all of eight acres of a managed wilderness of pools, reed beds, osiers and a jungle of chest-high willow herb, knitted together with dead bindweed. Each strand breaks easily, but 1,000 of them round your leg are like a hawser on the *Lusitania.*

We start off well enough in a wavy line. A typical shooting party comprises self and two sons armed, then brother-in-law laying about him with a stout cudgel, uttering shrill cries of encouragement. Next, a niece, straight from a fashion plate in Mr Purdey's catalogue, to whom a raindrop or spot of mud are as toxic waste: with squeaks of alarm, she skirts such hazards. Then, No. 1 Grandson with his unloaded, sawn-down air rifle next to his mother, who carries granddaughter on her back, a formidable *troika* ploughing doggedly through the rough. Then, comes the *Memsahib*, hair on end, encased in waterproofs, worrying about supper, next to my sister taking the line of least resistance, whacking away with the handle of an old golf club. Two fox terriers and two Labradors are in attendance, mostly out of sight, rampaging in the stalks.

Almost immediately, a woodcock flips up, three shots and it tumbles in the nettles. General ululation of approval, followed by long pause for the retrieve. Take a nip of sloe gin to celebrate. Next, a sprinkling of pheasants bursts from thrusting canine snouts, each eruption greeted with shouts of exhortation, grandson aims his airgun: a bird falls in the river, No. 1 Son's better dog swims to retrieve. A rabbit bolts along a ride, a snap shot and it tumbles. Legs trailing, a moorhen flutters tamely across the carp lake to collapse in a hail of pellets. Two more pheasants, a passing pigeon fluked down and then a teal, one of five, that catapult from the shallows. A skein of Canada geese honks over while a whiff of cigar smoke rises from the jungle. Beaters communicate with hooting cries like those rude pygmies in the Bolivian jungle, sung about by rugby clubs in amateur days, but at last we reach the big willow that marks the boundary. To comb eight acres took us an hour. One by one, like Wat Tyler's bedraggled army, we emerge, assembling by the tree to admire the bag: time for plum cake, hot soup and more sloe gin. There is much love, jollity and loud, critical analysis.

The shooters stay for the duck, while the rest go home to prepare a Lucullan feast of cold meats, bubble and squeak, home-pickled walnuts, beetroot, celery and a gigantic Stilton, decant the claret and pile the logs on the duck-basket grate. An hour after dark, the rest return, rosy-cheeked with four mallard and five more pigeons. They kick off boots, drinks are thrust into willing hands, ash logs glow and the curtains are drawn against the night. The roar of conversation is deafening.

It is self-indulgent, exclusive and selfish, but what the heck. For one day, we sidestep worries about multi-culturalism, political correctness, the neighbours, council bullies, the Government, speed cameras, foreign wars, official busybodies and the credit crunch, and reclaim a gentle way of life under threat. As long as the family Boxing Day potter survives, there will be a corner of an increasingly foreign field that is forever England.

Above: A peaceful pipe with Kenzie and Satch at Hunter's Fen.

Left: At Will Garfit's shoot at Hauxton.

Below: 4 fish – 1 rod. John, Peter, David and Max (with his first salmon) August 2011. A memorable day.

Above: The Humphreys family and dogs Hunter's Fen Boxing Day Shoot, 2006.

Left: Faithful China retrieves a partridge

Below: Broadlands Game Fair 1984, with his favourite goose head stick.

Above left: One of many happy days fishing at Grafham Water.

Above right: John, Max and David. Three generations at the Purdey award-winning Lords Ground Shoot.

Left: With fellow judge, The Duchess of Devonshire, at the Purdey Awards Presentation 2005.

Below: Netting tiddlers with Max and Madeline on the Tweed, 2008.

Above left: With the famous Roaring Emma, 2011.

Above right: Barbados 2004. John catches a Wahoo which featured on the hotel menu that night.

Left: A fine steelhead from the Muskegon River in snowy Michigan.

Below: With David in Peter's boat on the Muskegon River, Michigan.

Above: A proud grandfather with an 8 pound salmon and a 5½ pound grandson, Max.

Right: Another salmon, but Max weighs in heavier this time.

Below: A mixed bag, including a mouse from Hunter's Fen (David, John, Max and Peter).

Above: A good morning flight with Roaring Emma.

Left: Angela and John at a shoot and dog trial at Rainford Hall, Lancashire, October 2011.

Below: John's 70th birthday at Penbedw shoot, Flintshire. He wrote in his game diary 'Helluva day! Great reunion of many of the old Moor Gang.'

Above left: John loved hats and owned a variety of headgear; here he wears his Tilley Hat.

Above right: Receiving the 1995 Laurent Perrier Award for Lords Ground Shoot from HRH Prince Charles and the Duke of Wellington.

Left: Blowing his trumpet with Amadeus Boldwicket's Red Hot Peppers Jazz Band at a CLA Game Fair Shooting Times party.

Below: John with Angela – and trademark pipe – at the CLA Game Fair, Shuttleworth, 2001.

Above left: Pigeon shooting with China.

Above right: Morning flight with Tess.

Left: A proud shoot captain after Lords Ground won the Laurent Perrier Award for Wild Game Conservation.

Sporting Characters

*The characters in the shooting world are as much a
part of the scenery as the hedges, fields and
flightponds. John met a vast army of
shooting men and women in his career
as a writer. In this section are featured some
of the people he admired most and
some that he was fortunate enough
to call his friend.*

With hat and stick, 23 August 1984

*Every July, the CLA Game Fair caravan rolls into town at one of Britain's
more elaborate homes. Thousands flock to the show in homage to their
fieldsports. For John, the Game Fair was as important in the diary as the
Glorious Twelfth and it was the characters that made it, as this memorable
Country Gun column from 1984 shows.*

Many interesting things happened, but hats were the recurring
theme. A strange man approached as I was doing my
quacking act and asked me for a corncrake call. It took several
minutes of cautious badinage before I recognised a mischievous Peter
Whitaker [former deputy editor of *Shooting Times*] (without his Petrel
bowler hat) which was remiss of me as I had sat next to him at the
Shooting Times centenary lunch. Next, Roger Hum turned up with a
bandsman's marching hat, direct from New Orleans; a super present
for me, if rather inappropriate headwear for that particular occasion.
Then Allan Graham of Shooting Developments appeared in an
enormous, flat-brimmed straw, making him look like a giant, benign
mandarin; the Managing Editor elect of *Shooting Times* was sporting a
cool and snappy Panama; a South African banker came up wearing two
paper hats at once, one with the peak at the front, the other shielding
his neck, so clearly he found the Romsey climate every bit as hot as the
veldt. Archie Coats, on the other hand, was in his charcoal grey suit and
battered brown Derby – is he impervious to temperatures of eighty in
the shade? I noticed that the many clients who thronged the Eley stand
just to talk to the great man wore, on average, one item of clothing each
– very practical garb, given the conditions.

It was the Game Fair, of course, a hot one and clearly the time for
funny hats. The business was contagious for, on the Friday morning, I
crept off to Lock's and came out ten minutes later sheepishly wearing
a Panama (wise to keep in with the Managing Editor) and with a new
tweed shooting hat clutched in a brown paper bag. Last November I
left my best hat on a certain shooting lodge supper table in the
Cotswolds and have not seen it since. How ironic that, on the evening

of the very day of my purchase of a replacement, I should bump into Richard Fleming. "Got your hat, by the way," he said, "I'll post it to you when I get home". So, there are times when two heads are better than one, if only to serve as hatstands for two of Mr Lock's remarkable titfers. Whatever the weather holds in store next season, I shall be properly hatted!

I enjoyed this Fair, not least for the scores of fellow shooters who came up for a chat: each had an interesting story to relate. It was one of those times when I wished I had a tape recorder ready for instant action. Fowlers from Wigtown to the Wash, keepers, pigeon men and others made the three days a pleasant sojourn. I especially remember the Lakelander with his terrier. The dog was now an old, battle-worn pensioner with scars and ripped ears but a decidedly lively look in its rheumy eye. It was so ferocious that it bared its teeth at its master whom it loved; what it was like with strangers, I dreaded to think. The creature was no larger than a big rabbit but I kept my BASC table well between us.

Many young artists had some wonderful paintings on show. Will Garfit in linen suit and snap-brimmed straw hat, like Our Man in Havana, looked as cool and elegant as his work; Derick Bown's dead trees looked, if possible, even more ready for the axe, so realistic were they; Julian Novorol (bare headed) displayed his beloved punts and pinkfeet out on the mudflats while, a new name to me, Jonathan Yule had, in watercolour, captured the misty essence of his native North Norfolk coastal marshes, their people and birds. I hope to be able to review his work in more detail later in the year.

On other stands, Donald Downs of the Fly Fishers Guild (tweed porkpie) demonstrated his skills, while Theo Fossel (fore-and-aft with badges) dealt with a crowd of eager stick dressers and made many enrolments to his newly founded Stick Dressers Guild, an enterprise which is slowly but surely gaining momentum. Down at the clayground, the peaked baseball caps with straps at the back competed with Mike Alldis' shorts for attention; at *Shooting Times*, Coin Willock, Fred Taylor and Geoffrey Boothroyd (all hatless) were in evidence. I had a quick word with Major Bruce Kinloch, also bare headed, for his many years under tropical skies had enabled this inveterate globetrotter and big game hunter to scorn the feeble sun of an English summer. For the rest, there were knotted handkerchiefs, folded newspapers, battered straws with faded regimental or old school favours, bush hats, tweeds, felts, flat caps, deerstalkers and boaters. For me, Broadlands Game Fair will de remembered as the year of the hat.

However, there is more, for I will remember it also as the year of the stick and the occasion or a most amazing stroke of luck against incalculable odds. Like many countrymen, I have a favourite stick. The handle is a pinkfoot goose head with a staghorn neck, exquisitely carved by that master decoy carver Roger Jeeves. The stick itself is a woodbine, a straight hazel which the constricting vice of a spiralling honeysuckle had deeply grooved into a striking barleysugar twist. Not that uncommon, perhaps, but I cut it from a Wiltshire copse in which, many years ago, I shot my first roebuck. I used it for years for beating, for leaning on and as a faithful companion on happy days too numerous to recall. One day I whacked playfully at a stout teazle behind which an iron post lurked and the lower third of my beloved stick flew off into oblivion.

Now it was a short stick, too short, in fact and Theo Fossel of the aforementioned Stick Dressers Guild took it away and carried out a neat transplant, grafting on a piece of hazel below the fracture so that the join was indiscernible. The stick was now fit only for Game Fairs and strolling round on holiday. A 'Sunday stick' and definitely not for chastising boys or dogs or bashing the brambles. It holds, as many sticks do, a very special place in my affection.

At the Game Fair I leaned it on my table, turned my back to talk to a visitor and looked round a moment later to find it gone. An opportunist thieving dacoit had stolen it. I felt that cold clutch in the vitals, that sinking feeling which leaves you sick and oozing self-pity, but it was my own fault, of course. The Fair was at its busiest, a solid throng of irritable, sweating people, jammed in the avenues, heaving back and forth. Dear Sid Semark set off and walked up and down trying to spot the stick. I did likewise in the opposite direction, but what possible chance was there? None at all. My Game Fair was ruined; I grew morose, miserable and preoccupied. I told my wife and tears sprang to her eyes for she knew what the old stick meant to me. I even thought of positioning myself at the exit to the Fair and scanning every visitor on his way to the car park, but there were many exits and it would have been like searching for one grain of wheat in a 50-acre field of corn.

Now comes the incredible part of the tale. For some reason Theo Fossel, the man who had repaired my stick, decided on a whim to leave his busy Four Shot stand in order to visit a standholder on the other side of the avenue. He battled against the press of humanity; it was the busy time of a hectic day and he, the one man in the 50,000 present who had repaired it, bumped bang into the one man in 50,000 present who had stolen it. Theo did not know my stick was lost; he could have passed by, convincing himself that it had been come by legitimately. To his eternal credit, he confronted the person who claimed to have bought it. Eventually Theo suggested they had a word with the nearby policeman and that was the end of it. Triumphantly clutching the spoils of war, like the good chap he is, he came hurrying up to me at the BASC with the news.

All was well again and friends calling "Got your stick?" each time I made a move and suggesting I attach it to my person with a long string could not dull my deep sense of relief and gratitude to Theo. When I had told anyone who would listen of the great service he had done me, even Lock's would have had nothing big enough to fit him!

Wild wings and some footsteps, 27 January 1983

A legend in the wildfowling world, Jimmy Wentworth Day was a romantic, a conservative with both a small and big 'C', a ghost hunter and an incongruous figure in the modern age. In 1983, John wrote this obituary to one of the shooting world's liveliest characters.

It was two years ago that I saw him for the last time, a slight, dapper figure in whipcord breeches, yellow waistcoat, sports coat and spotted handkerchief with that aggressively bristling moustache and pebble glasses which have peered out defiantly from the dust jackets of so many books. He was almost completely blind but in that, his eightieth year, he had shot a driven pheasant by firing at the sound of its wings. At dinner he was a wonderful raconteur, leaping to his feet to emphasise a story, gesticulating and imitating perfectly the accents of Duke, butler and Essex farm labourer. Winston Churchill had damned his eyes on the steps of the Athenaeum; Lord Beaverbrook had hired and fired him; he wrote millions of words, the very first, for which he received no payment, appearing in *Shooting Times* when he was still a teenager.

Born in Exning, Suffolk on 21 April 1899, the son of J.T. Wentworth Day and boasting numerous famous and notorious ancestors – thorns in the flesh of authority to a man – he was a youngster when, to use his own words, 'the East Anglian firmament was full of shooting stars', and he fitted perfectly into the world in which he found himself. At his home in Wicken, his family owned Adventurers Fen, the last remnant of the old Fen of Hereward and haunt of swallowtails, harriers, bitterns, countless wildfowl and little, wild marsh pheasants. During the Second World War his beloved marsh was drained by the 'War Ag' whom Jimmy never forgave for what he considered a monumental piece of bureaucratic vandalism. The marsh was subsequently reflooded and made into a National Trust reserve, but for James it had lost its wild magic. Later he moved to Essex, fell in love with it and made it his home.

As a boy he was often to be found in the company of the local poachers, fishermen, fowlers, dyke-diddlers and Fen slodgers. His first gun, a single barrel percussion converted from flint, was confiscated by his father and thrown into the river on account of the too many hours it was felt James spent in its company. He often spoke with regret of its loss but he had already learned to love the wild places, the creatures that flew, ran and swam there and the sport that was to be had with them. A natural flair for words and the ability to communicate the incommunicable brought the marshes, coverts and the extravagant characters who haunted them into thousands of suburban lounges.

He had a passion for ghosts of which East Anglia boasts more than its share. I walked a dark lane with him one night while he, an anachronistic figure in reach-me-down brown overcoat, curly brimmed brown bowler, silver-topped cane and the usual yellow waistcoat, told me the tale of Black Shuck, the great spectral hound of Spinney Bank, to see which meant death within the week. Such was his way with words and the magic of his storytelling that more than once, I found myself glancing nervously over my shoulder. He wrote three books on ghosts and lectured to packed halls on the subject.

While he had met and shot with some of the legendary names of the covert-side, wildfowling was his great love. In the 1920s he was the founder of the London branch of WAGBI, founder and chairman of the Essex Wildfowlers' Association from which he '…resigned in disgust owing to the number of non-wildfowlers, totally ignorant of the sport, who wished to join in order to find out where they might get free shooting.' He was also an Hon. Life member of WAGBI, to which he was elected for past services to the sport. His book *The Modern Fowler*, first published in 1934 and since reprinted, was a standard work on the subject, remarkable for its blend of hard fact and romance, its linking of saltmarsh Vikings with the 'rum owd boys' who lived there now. Few could have known the east coast fowling and fowlers in the 1930s better than he.

In his time, he rented some of the best duck marshes in England, including Salthouse Broad and Burnley Hall Estate in Norfolk and also the famous Old Hall Marshes in Essex. He knew every gunner worth knowing and had been out with many of them punting, flight shooting and absorbing their tales which he lovingly reproduced and, let it be whispered, sometimes enhanced in his writings. As a journalist he was bath volatile and versatile and had occupied important positions in *Country Life, The Field, The Illustrated Sporting* and *Dramatic News* and a number of Fleet Street dailies. For a time he was editor and owner of *Saturday Review* which he used to alert the apathetic British public to the dangers of German rearmament in the 1930s. Almost to his death he wrote a regular countryside column in *The Daily Mail.* An ardent Royalist, he wrote the official biography of George V as a sportsman: the King said of him, 'This chap knows what he's talking about.' He also researched and wrote the biography of Princess Marina, Duchess of Kent and more lately wrote *The Queen Mother's Family Story.* He wrote on all manner of subjects from the life of Sir Donald Campbell to a forgotten corner of an Essex wood with the same flamboyant, trenchant style, felicitous turn of phrase and happy knack of painting instantly recognisable word pictures. The series of which *Sporting Adventure* and *Farming Adventure* are two was especially well regarded, sold many thousands of copies and fired goodness knows how many readers with a love of wild sports and the English countryside.

He was an incurable romantic, some would say a romancer, but his evocation of the slumbering lust of the crawling tideway with its echoes of Danish raiders in their longships, or the unshaven ghosts of the Roman garrison at Canvey Island, could touch the heart of the most hard-bitten reader. I owe much of my own love of such things to James' writing, for his books read when I was a schoolboy first opened my mind to the wild adventure of longshore fowling, and my eyes to the beauties of my own Cambridgeshire. I will be one of many to have been thus affected.

His politics were somewhat to the right of Attilla the Hun and his outspoken, forthright views expressed in devastating prose did not endear him to the enemies who gather round any trenchant, abrasive personality. He routed Conrad Noel, the 'red' vicar of Thaxted, burning his red flag and forcing him to preach a sermon under the Union Jack he had insulted. A Liverpool mob chased him down the street when he asked an unanswerable question of Emmanuel Shinwell; of Ted Heath he said, 'too much paunch and not enough punch.' He listed under his recreations, 'taking the Left Wing intelligentsia at its own valuation'. In *Farming Adventure* he wrote, 'The trouble with intellectuals is that they are so seldom intelligent, frequently perverts and almost invariably conceited'. Of wild boar he wrote, 'They smelled sweeter than the Russians who were on the other side of the forest'. He wore his prejudices on his sleeve and such barbs – and there are many of them – did not endear him to his targets. Far from worrying about controversy, he revelled in it and once even challenged an enemy to a duel.

He saw service in two World Wars, once as war correspondent, was an important witness in the famous Harold Laski libel action of 1946, enjoyed the patronage of Lady Houston, the richest woman in England, and twice stood for Parliament, slashing the Hornchurch Socialist majority in the elections of 1950 and 1951. He was a man of his time, champion of lost causes and epitome of the Edwardian squire who liked to 'live as my fathers lived in the days ere I was born'. His love of long guns, good horses, honest dogs, straight talking and the wild places were absolutely genuine and when coupled with his naturally evocative style of writing, such things made irresistible material.

He was 83 when he died, an extraordinary, rumbustuous, colourful character, a latter-day Whig, an echo of a lost age and somehow an incongruous figure in today's grey, drab Britain. His proper place was standing next to Harry Stoner as the Elveden pheasants poured over, browsing with George V in the Sandringham gunroom or out with wizened Walter Linnett in the punt after brent on the Blackwater.

At our last meeting he overwhelmed me by inviting me to write his obituary, 'but don't be in too much of a hurry old chap'. How can one do justice to 83 overflowing years in so few words? The task and the man call for a Surtees at the very least. I hope he would not have been offended by my words for they come from the heart; James would be a formidable ghost with whom to live. He did express the wish that a few old gunners up and down the land would raise a glass to his memory. I add my hope that they will do so, for we will not look upon his like again.

King of the Essex gunners, 7 February 2008

Fifty years after Walter Linnet died in the same shack in which he was born, John Humphreys headed back to the Essex saltmarshes to unearth the ghosts of fowlers past.

There is an old spiritual we used to play in the band named 'Walking with the King'. A while back, I too walked in the footsteps of royalty, not any old king but the king of the Essex wildfowlers. His name was Walter Linnet. He died in 1958, in the cottage in which he was born. It was a three-roomed, single-storey, barge-boarded shack on the edge of the saltings; at high tide you could stand on his front porch and spit into the sea. The rent was £6.50 pa. His gunning punt was moored in the appropriately named Gunners' Creek, out front where most people have begonias. When he saw a paddling of fowl or stand of plover he would pole out, using the wind and sun to make a shot. Otherwise he would prowl with his hammergun seeking small birds valuable for collectors, pulling samphire, raking cockles, spearing flatties, setting lines or picking oysters from his oyster bed. The duck he wrapped in brown paper and sent by post to an eminent surgeon in London, Mrs Linnet making the trip for the post office.

His own family ate wigeon or mallard only as a special treat at Christmas, the rest of their protein coming from flock shots at 'oxbirds' (dunlin) and other small waders. Not for nothing were godwits a corruption of the old Saxon 'good-to-eat' while 'olives' were oystercatchers, named after St Olaf. These, Mrs L made into the fail-safe 'oystercock pudden' to feed the family. It worked well enough, for on a diet of waders, flat fish and a few spuds the Linnets brought up six children in a cottage so small that one good leap would carry you the width of the main room. Walter died in his eighties and his wife in her nineties. Their water came not even from a well but from running land drains from the fields behind.

Linnet's father lived in that very place, built in 1798 at a cost of £165, and he followed the same trade as his father and his son, taking part in the great punt shot at 740 Brent, on St Peter's Point nearby, in 1861.

Within a gunshot of the cottage stands what is said to be the oldest church in England, St Peter's Chapel on the Wall, dedicated to St Cedd (sometimes St Chad), who travelled down the coast from Northumberland to convert the heathens of Essex. To this day the question remains, did he succeed? The church was built in 653AD from stones of the great Roman fort of Othona on the same site, one of a dozen that dotted the lonely marshes protecting the east coast. The original arches are still there and round the six-acre perimeter runs the wall, now half-buried, that kept out the raiding Saxon hooligans. The church was once used as a smugglers' store and what a perfect place for the gentlemen of the night to keep their booty. Owls nested in it and a peregrine roosted on the roof, digesting the latest gull. It may be that there were Saxon Linnets there in the time of 'Thim owd Roomans', for Wentworth Day was convinced that his blue eyes and straw-coloured hair spoke of those wild invaders.

What a place for a solitary fowler to live, wild and lonely, the spume of the waves at high tide bleaching the front door and splashing the roof tiles. Linnet was ever distrustful of things of the land, only eating fruit of the sea. He cared not for chickens, being land birds, and his spud patch he set on the seaward side of the wall so that his few tatties might be said to have come from the tide. I never met him but they spoke of a long, lean man, brown as a herring, his manner quiet and shy, suspicious of strangers and rarely going into his village of Bradwell-juxta-Mare. They said he went each year to the flower show and others recalled that once a week he walked up the High Street to buy an ounce of shag tobacco. It was said that people withdrew into their houses and children hid when he marched with measured tread along the middle of the road, like the old gunslinger in 'High Noon'. Curtains twitched and dogs made themselves scarce.

The reason I appear so knowledgeable on the subject is because my pal Julian Novorol, one of the finest fowlers and artists on the coast, took me on a pilgrimage to the cottage and cathedral. It was a long drag round the River Crouch but we found the place and tramped the long walk down to the marsh. I thought of Mrs Linnet carrying all those duck and of Walter on his tobacco run. The wind was sharp and salty, squadrons of Brent croaked and flapped along the tide and clouds of knot whirred like electric butterflies along the mud. The tide was high and there stood the cottage, tarred boards and a weatherbeaten roof. Peering through the window I saw a sagging easy chair by a black iron grate; one could picture Walter taking his ease before a fire of driftwood, children clustered round his knees.

Julian had another advantage – he had been invited to the pub and interviewed one of Walter's surviving sons, the late Walter Thomas, known as 'Tucker', who told him about life in the old cottage. Today it was quiet save for a covey of birdwatchers with woolly hats and telescopes getting excited about a fall of little auks driven down the coast by foul weather. They were kind and told us many things about the old place. The tide slid back, we sploshed out and with our backs to the sea, gazed at the cottage, much as it had been, even the poles marking the oyster bed remained. Behind the house where the suspect chickens and veg were reared was self-set scrub birch and elder and a few fruit trees left over from Linnet's day. It took little imagination to picture Walter poling his punt or hauling his lines.

The 'cathedral' was built of stones first used to keep weather and invader away from Caesar's legions in the fort and it too was full of ghosts. It showed signs of many repairs but the tall, austere building withstood the rage of the East winds as it had for centuries and there were rows of plain pews and a simple altar to show that it was used for its original purpose. Between Linnet's cottage and the church was the old wall laid bare by rabbits and erosion. I stooped and took a piece of red Roman tile, detached and lying loose in the earth, a scrap the size of a fag packet and about as thick, and slipped it in my pocket. As mother would have said, 'If we all did that there would be nothing left,' but I took it anyway and squeezed it in my hand as if to wring from it a picture of the man who made it and what it had beheld during two millennia.

It was a pilgrimage all fowlers ought to take. Linnet lived by hard work and his wits. There was no National Assistance, no state gave him a heating allowance and, should his gun misfire, his spear fail or his net break, his family went hungry. To speak in the same breath of Linnet and his life as a fowler, and modern 'sportsmen' who shoot 100 geese on a field, shows it to be the greedy obscenity it is.

It was lunchtime and we left the slumbering marshland with its two historic outposts dreaming of past glories and went to the Green Man pub, where the punters who made that monstrous shot at Brent in 1861 went to celebrate. I could imagine the fug of cheap tobacco smoke, the roar of voices, the spilled beer, the flagged floor and the crowds, Walter's old father among them. Just down the lane crawled the creek where they moored their punts. They said that in the next room was a table where in the old days they laid out the dead bodies – it doubled as the village mortuary.

I doubt I will ever return, but it was a visit that had to be made while I still was able. In Linnet's cottage, Roaring Emma was a frequent visitor, as was James Wentworth Day and other gunners and scribes of times past. Julian and I had joined those who had come to the shrine. Without a backward glance we turned away from that strange place and tramped inland along the green Roman road; we had some descendants of Linnet's duck to shoot.

Ghost of a chance, 21 April 2005

Sometimes fate plays out in such an extraordinary way that you can't help but wonder at the intervention of a higher power, as did John when he recounted this story of his friend Graham Wilson, back in 2005.

By and large there is a general shortage of ectoplasm in the shooting world – nothing much spooky tends to happen and most out-of-body experiences may be attributed to too much sloe gin. I did hear a yarn from Essex that people swear is true but you may judge for yourselves. An old fowler in the muzzle-loading days was the quickest reloader ever seen – his secret was not to use powder and shot flasks but to keep his powder loose in his right-hand pocket, his shot in his left. He was pretty slick at snatching just the right amount of powder in a clenched fist and throwing it down the muzzle. People came miles to see him in action. It all went pear-shaped one day when in the heat of the moment he took his pipe from his mouth and stuffed it still alight into his right-hand jacket pocket. They say the resulting pyrotechnics were spectacular and his ghost haunted the marshes thereafter on nights of pale moon and mist, seen most often by fowlers who had just come out of the pub.

He was the only ghoul on the block until I heard from my pal Graham Wilson, a distinguished director and manager of Henry Monk, the renowned provincial gunsmith and sporting emporium in Queen Street, Chester. Graham is a genial, level-headed cove not liable to imaginative turns and his story I found quite eerie. As a spotty 15-year-old back in the 1960s he was about to leave school and, with little enthusiasm, was contemplating his future. His dad had got him fixed up as a plasterer with the local firm where his brother worked, but the prospects of wielding a trowel for the next 50 years were not appealing. In the weeks leading up to him leaving school he would often cycle with some mates out to the village of Great Barrow, where they sat in a row on the churchyard wall chewing the fat, putting the world to rights and wondering anxiously about their futures, as adolescents do.

The boys discussed their impending launch into the grown-up world and the uncertainties that lay ahead. The more Graham thought about plastering, the less appealing it sounded. His dad was sympathetic and in the paper happened upon a Henry Monk advertisement asking for staff. Graham did a bit of shooting with a rusty .410 and often filled his mother's larder, so this sounded a bit more like it. He went for interview, was accepted for the post and has been there ever since, happy, fulfilled and largely responsible for making the business the success it has become. The job was tailor-made for him. Over the years, promotion came and he developed an interest in the Monk history, did some research but was never able to find the family grave, a worrying loose end. Then an old fowling pal telephoned excitedly to say that he had stumbled on the gravestone in a neighbouring village churchyard.

After work, Graham dashed to St Bartholomew's churchyard at Great Barrow, hunted around and found the grave of the Monk family. The hairs on the back of his neck stood up and for a moment he was rooted to the spot, for it lay within a few feet of the very wall where, back in 1965, he had sat swinging his legs, pondering his future. He could have leaned over and touched it. Had a ghostly hand reached out from beyond the grave and tapped him gently on the shoulder, directing him towards a profession and to a firm where he has been nothing but happy? He stared at the gravestone and noticed the date of Henry Monk's death: 4 May 1941. Graham's birthday is on 4 May.

The hard-nosed and unimaginative might cry 'coincidence', but I prefer the more interesting explanation. There were many other villages the boys might have visited, so what took them to Great Barrow? There were hundreds of places they might have sat, so why choose the churchyard wall? The wall was long and they could have sat anywhere along its length, so what made them sit almost on top of the grave? Of the scores of places the lad might have gone to work, why did it have to be Monk's? It was many years before Graham realised the significance of what had happened and that he needed Monk's as much as Monk's needed him – *There is destiny that shapes our ends...*

Give us old romantics the benefit of the doubt and admit that it is at least, a very curious story.

Stanley Duncan, 16 June 1983

To wildfowlers and long-standing readers of **Shooting Times,** *Stanley Duncan needs no introduction. The founder of the Wildfowlers' Association, he was a true visionary of the shooting world. John wrote this biographical piece on Duncan in the 75th anniversary year of the association he founded.*

To many, the name of Stanley Duncan and his tarred, black wildfowling hut at Patrington Haven are part of the folklore of shooting. We may know little enough about either of them, save the one important fact that Duncan had founded WAGBI and that his hut was the shrine in which he and a few like-minded spirits discussed the future of their sport. This, the 75th year of what became BASC, is as good a time as any for a backward glance, to remember our fragile beginnings and reflect on the tough and resilient man who started the whole thing off.

Stanley Duncan was born in the last quarter of the 19th century and he spent most of his life in Hull. He could trace his family on his mother's side to Dawney, the Victorian court photographer, but his stock was yeoman, he himself working all his life as an engineer on the LNER. His father was no shot but he took young Stanley out often enough to fire the boy with a love of wild places and the fowl which haunted them. Shore gunning was unrestricted: there was little legislation regarding close seasons or protected species. If you encountered a rare bird, you took Sir Ralph Payne Gallwey's advice and shot it before the next gun beat you to it; then you sold it to one of the naturalists of the day. Shore shooting consisted of walking the marshes, and if you saw a bird, be it shore lark, gull, dunlin or owl, you shot it. On arrival, your first act would be to hurry down to the tide to recover any cripples or dead birds lost by the many punters, professional and amateur, who worked the estuary. To shoot a duck or a goose was a matter for celebration.

Duncan did his share of this in his early days and even after he had founded WAGBI, godwits, ruffs, owls, herons and even a kingfisher featured in his bag. His keenness made him eager for better things and he built permanent hides, ('huts' he called them), made stuffed decoys and became a highly proficient caller of fowl, especially curlew and wigeon. In such ways he showed himself to be a man ahead of his time. He kept notes of his trips, understanding the importance of records, writing them mostly in his LNER notebook and also on the back of an envelope or any other scrap of paper which came to hand. These records are preserved in the BASC archives and they make fascinating reading. Additional information comes from his friend and disciple, Trevor Field who recorded his outings with Duncan in the 1930s. The paper he wrote on the subject is essential reading for anyone researching the life of the great man. Duncan emerges from it as a rugged, four-square individual with weather-beaten, brown face, easy-going and phlegmatic, but a fearsome figure when enraged, such as when he discovered that a farmer had padlocked his access gate to the marsh. The farmer was lucky to escape with a verbal drubbing; only a deep creek between them prevented bloodshed. As a shot he was slow and deliberate. The youthful Field would empty his gun into the geese with no effect, but Duncan's measured *bang, pause, bang,* followed by two thumps in the mud, were hallmarks of his shooting.

The famous hut was built at home, taken down a section at a time and erected on the marsh above the high-water mark. It was neat and snug with a stove, basic cooking facilities, a bunk for Duncan and a blanket on the floor for guests. A candle on a shelf provided illumination, many a Homeric fry-up and animated conversation was enjoyed there while the wind roared outside. The curlew, shore birds and the odd wigeon were hung on a row of nails under the eaves. After many years, the hut blew down in a gale and was washed away.

Duncan was not content to be a 'shore-popper' all his life. His farmer friends inland invited him partridge and rabbit shooting; he pursued the pinkfeet up on the Wolds, decoyed pigeons, and discovered punt gunning. He evolved a conversion system for making ML guns into BL guns; he designed and built 13 punts, keeping a single and a double down on the shore, ready for action. He kept his gear meticulously and would not set out unless he was certain that he had everything in tip-top order. He was not a big bag man, but over the years he killed grey geese, brent, curlew, mallard and wigeon in a series of exciting stalks.

He was adopted by *Shooting Times* as its gun expert and wrote for the magazine for 50 years. The editor was Arthur Bonsall who became vice-president of the infant WAGBI, and his magazine has been a staunch ally ever since. Duncan was sent guns to test, especially by Fords, the noted Birmingham gunmaker; he tested the prototype of the famous BSA magnum as well as a 3-in 20-bore 'Midget Magnum' which Fords made to his specification. He was also an expert at identifying rare species while his *Jotting for Wildfowlers* and handling of readers' queries in *Shooting Times* was a popular feature. He was made a Fellow of the Zoological Society for his services to natural history, a proper recognition that the shooter could also be an ornithologist and yet another example of Duncan's anticipating future trends.

Another of his enthusiasms was photography and within the severe limitations of the cumbersome plate camera, he recorded bags, places and people, and many boxes of his glass negatives are still extant. He was also an artist and his sketches often illustrated his writings, notably his *magnum opus, The Complete Wildfower, Ashore and Afloat* which he wrote in conjunction with Guy Thorne. This has become a standard work on the subject, especially where punting is concerned, for he covers it in minute detail. He once was sent for appraisal and comment some bird pictures from a young student called Peter Scott.

With Sir Ralph Payne Gallwey as president, Duncan as secretary and his fowling pals from Hull on the committee, the inaugural meeting of the Wildfowlers' Association was held in the Imperial Hotel, Hull in April 1908. The object was to protect the interests of shore gunners and to combat adverse publicity; hostile farmers and erosion of the habitat – by 1908 pollution, for example, was already becoming a worry.

For years after, the ten-shilling subscription proved hard to collect; gunners tended to be apathetic and two World Wars caused the Association almost to flounder. At one point, amalgamation with the BFSS (itself a spin-off of the early WAGBI) was proposed but voted against in a poll of all the members. Only Duncan's determination saw WAGBI through the lean years until, in the 1950s, he passed the burden on to younger shoulders and, under John Anderton OBE and his team, the steady trickle of the converted became a flood.

Natural History

As befits a winner of the Laurent Perrier award for game conservation, John's knowledge of flora and fauna was extensive. From his earliest years, natural history was a passion and it was a subject that he loved to write on and share, as this selection of articles demonstrates.

Action stations, 9 April 1992

Hunter's Fen, a seven-acre patch of Cambridgeshire, is more than simply a plot of land. It is where John brought to life his dream of a pocket-handkerchief wild bird shoot. This article from 1992 outlines the naturalist's manifesto he implemented there.

One of my little schoolmasterly indulgences is to ask of my scholars a definition of the word 'green'. They tell me it is the colour of grass and young leaves and urge me but to look out of the window to see acres of examples. In the end I tease out of them with didactic charm a blend of Mr Chips and Plato, that green is not a colour but a word of five letters beginning with the letter G.

How do they know that what they see and call green is what I see? For all we know it might be to them what I call purple, but green it was called from their mother's knee so green it becomes. Until medical science releases upon us the full head transplant, we will never be able to see through the eyes of another, so a great mystery remains; in the meantime, who cares?

Much the same is true of the word 'conservation'. We stumble across well-meaning folk in pubs, school playgrounds, offices, on farms and in the outer suburbs who, when asked of their interests, roll their eyes heavenwards like a saint in the bottom corner of a stained glass window and whisper in reverent tones, "I'm very much into conservation, actually."

Like green, conservation is but a word and it has come to mean many things to many folk. None of them do I decry, including those who join pressure groups to prevent official vandalism of ancient meadows, write passionately to the paper about unkindnesses to frogs, design posters and stick them on the parish notice board, parade with banners, save their old newspapers or deliver sermons to bemused schoolchildren about the ozone layer.

All have their place and count as acceptable definitions of the big C, but they are not mine. When someone tells you they are passionately into conservation, ask to look at their hands. The one for my money has blisters and callouses caused by hours with a spade, heaving buckets or lugging potted saplings down to a forgotten corner.

This person will not be at many meetings – he will be out doing it rather than talking about it. His back might he stooped from carrying heavy loads and if he gives you access to his bank account there will be regular withdrawals for tools, chemicals, trees, plants, petrol and materials.

Look at his car: it will speak of muddy lanes and having its cargo area filled with more than just shopping. There will be dents in the bodywork, missing wing mirrors, dry mud in the back and old wellies lying deflated but ever-ready in the boot.

Conservation ought to be mainly about doing, not talking. I have no more energy than the next man and a lot less than many, but my own little slice of heaven – Hunter's Fen, seven acres of forgotten real estate in the Cambridgeshire fens – has known my tender loving care for a decade.

It all started through pure self-interest, as I wanted to make my own shoot. In year one there was habitat for little more than a snipe, and several wigeon might drop in when the floods were up. The rough grass and close-cropped rush were pockmarked with the hooves of countless bullocks and that was it.

To make it shootable, I had to get stuck in. This I did with little planning at first, but the learning curve steepened as I got the hang of things and one timorous thought led to a bolder one. The first one-acre pond was dug; it has been re-dug and cleaned out twice since and will need another quick dredge next year. Its shapes, contours, varying depths, islands and shallows were lovingly planned; the digger driver, nagged to a nervous wreck, was skimming here, gouging there, and grading the soil elsewhere.

In one year it blended as though it had been there forever. Duck found it, as did frogs – helped by annual implants from me – plus newts, water spiders and myriad other insects. There were short-eared owls, hen harriers, kingfishers and water rails – all homed in not to live but to rest, feed and pass on.

Plants were set, although this was quite unnecessary as they came in by themselves and then the problem was too much growth. Every spring became an assault course of pruning and slashing, leading into a summer of aching shoulders when the scythe and knapsack sprayer opened rides and kept the weeds from overhanging the margins and covering up the duck loafing areas. Too much weed in the water meant more scything, suffering the prickly heat of breast-high waders for days on end and dragging the cut rubbish onto the bank.

Then came a time of planting little trees – more long-term commitment because, seven years later, the weeds need clearing from their trunks and rabbits must be kept at bay. Others helped, local conservationists with nowhere to conserve, schoolchildren and friends were all sucked into the scheme and I could not have done it without them. A small strip of gamecover was drilled on the drier part, scarecrows were needed at the right time and more rabbits needed thinning out. Every tool, bale, post and sack was carried, for no vehicle could get anywhere near.

Little extras included the siting and building of discreet hides for shooting, cutting out secret pathways through the jungle carrying straw and corn, setting little seats in the rushes and the introduction of some mighty carp.

The latter may not be good for the frogs, toads and insects but one cannot have everything and I happen to prefer the everyday pleasure of the feeding carp to the fleeting sight of a frog. Anyway, they have to be very voracious carp indeed to eat all the frogs and all the insects. Mine are well fed on surplus school bread.

What set out as trailblazing became maintenance. Every year the willow slips I planted with such abandon in the early days need pollarding, the bankside weed needs controlling, hides need trimming, duck and fish fed almost daily.

Conservation becomes damned hard, physical work, not a fleeting visit, job done and forgotten, but every week of the year, a task – and that on a pocket handkerchief of seven acres. To me, conservation is 10 percent inspiration, 90 per cent perspiration.

The result is a micro shoot which has produced 100 wild pheasants and 100 wild duck in a season, and that is taking it steady. The rewards are many and diverse and the resident wildlife a joy – the more so when I get that buzz from reflecting immodestly that I did it; without me it would be nothing.

When the next do-gooder corners you and professes a passion for conservation, look out for his or her blisters and reflect that, when all is said and done, there's a lot more said than done.

Hawks and Handsaws, 19 March 1981

Frequently John wrote in depth about the animals and birds that inhabit the natural world he so cherished. In this feature from **Shooting Times**, *the heron's place in life and literature is examined.*

When Hamlet scoffs at Polonius and tells him he cannot distinguish between a hawk and a handsaw, he was not referring to that familiar and useful tool of the woodwork bench. The line is easily interpreted by any Norfolk farm labourer. For centuries, the heron or heronshaw has been called in that county a Jack Hanser or simply as the hanser. A simple blend of hanser and heronshaw gives us handsaw, and so the object of Hamlet's derision was claimed to be unable to distinguish between the two birds. At the time, this would have been no light insult, as falcons were commonly flown at herons which gave good sport; heron plumes were, and still are, favourite adornments for falcon hoods. An inability to tell the hunter from the hunted would have indicated a surprising depth of ignorance amounting to lunatic senility – the precise point about his prospective father-in-law which the harassed Prince of Denmark was keen to make.

Nowadays, hawks and handsaws are spared each other's attentions and I doubt if encounters in the wild occur as often as blue moons, although I dare say that now and then a peregrine will try a half-hearted, playful stoop. Both species seem to have increased in number over the last ten years. The heron has always been a bird of the Fen country and it is a rare journey through the flat lands on which you do not see at least one. Slowing down to crawling speed at the bridges over the dykes and drains – and what true countryman can resist a glance up and down every waterway he crosses? – will often reveal a heron. He stands like a streak of bleached rushes, sometimes he looks grey, sometimes white, depending how the light catches him, but invariably he stands motionless. He waits for his prey to come to him, his cold yellow eye gazing intently at the water round his ankles. He is no neurotic spoonbill or egret, forever striding about, stirring up the mud and snapping the creatures disturbed. Jack Heron is a model of repose, of patience and of philosophy, very like the human inhabitants and the scenery of the places he haunts.

However, let a shoal of small roach or, better still, an eel come within range, and that emaciated, ragged bundle of grey dusters is transformed into a striking cobra, a steel spring, a bolt from a crossbow. Biding his time, waiting for the perfect range and instinctively allowing for refraction, the poiniard of a bill darts into the water with a speed which defies the human eye. There are lessons for the wildfowler in his methods of hunting. The next moment, the squirming eel is held aloft. In vain it threshes and wraps itself round the head and neck of its captor. With a dextrous flick, the eel is turned head-on and swallowed alive. Tiny serrations inside the heron's throat help to keep it down, but in the case of larger specimens, a few inches of feebly waving tail may, for some minutes, remain protruding from the side of the heron's bill.

For such a sagacious bird, it will often strike at more than it can swallow. Trout of some pounds' weight are stabbed with surgical deftness with a single blow on the back of the head. Often the stricken fish will escape but sometimes it is dragged ashore and, in the case of hen fish, the roe only is eaten. Dabs in tidal estuaries are a favourite prey and they must provide a bold target at which to aim. Water rats, moorhen chicks, moles and, I fear, mallard ducklings are not immune from attack. Frogs were once a favourite food but they are now rare indeed in our county in places where once they dwelt in thousands.

The proliferation of fish farms and small private trout fisheries has given the heron a large and attractive new larder. Wires are cunningly set to trip his spindly shanks, nets are stretched over stews and angry fishery owners lurk in the bushes with shotguns. Even so, you have to be up early to catch old Nog. He has been and gone ere your early morning tea is brewed. He is protected by Law, but the usual escape clause about fish-pond robbers pertains, and he may be punished for proven damage should all other deterrents have been tried and failed. The heron's undoing is that once he has found a good place, he sticks to it until he has cleared it. Even garden fish ponds are not safe and my neighbour's goldfish were cruelly mopped-up early one morning while he lay abed. Such a raid requires a good deal of courage on the part of the heron. His innate terror of human beings leads to a natural caution which makes an expedition into the very camp of the enemy a matter for considerable circumspection.

This phobia of humans is exploited in a trick once practised by Norfolk farm boys. A lad would creep up to the heron as close as he could: this was no mean feat, as the heron rarely settled where he could not command a good view of the approaches. If the boy was skilful or lucky enough to squirm, undetected, to within a few feet of his victim, he would suddenly leap out with a mighty shout and waving of his arms. The heron's nervous system received such a traumatic shock that it promptly fell down in a faint and could be easily bagged. That, at least, is how Norfolk old-timers describe it to me and I am sure that they would not, knowingly, exaggerate.

Heronries, like rookeries, have suffered through the scourge of Dutch elm disease which killed most of the favourite nesting trees. However, heronries come, flourish and move elsewhere in different sorts of trees, and it is my view that they have waxed despite the rather unfavourable breeding conditions. The smelly and rickety nests, plastered with guano and fish bones and protecting broods of unlovely, querulous youngsters, are not pretty sights to the layman but to the ornithologist they are places of consuming interest and, for old Nog, they are home.

We have quite a number of herons on our shoot and I often see two or three together, standing mournfully in the middle of a naked field of winter drill, the cutting wind stirring their feathers like the plumes on an admiral's dress hat. So often are they there, many hundreds of yards from the nearest water, that I can only assume they are digesting and contemplating. There cannot be anything there to eat – or can there?

Hawks, and falcons too, have been on the increase lately, and there are favourable reports of peregrines, ospreys, golden eagles and even sea-eagles. Our shoot has its share of kestrels, each pair to its own territory, and it has become a regular milestone on motorway journeys to see one swooping and hovering above the grassy banks. One recent encounter with a raptor: I was doing the rounds of the shoot, topping-up the feed hoppers when a bird which, at first glance, could have been a pigeon or a gull, drifted across the drove in front of me. It was dove grey and there was some white on it but a second look made for instant recognition. It was a cock hen harrier in all the finery of his mature plumage, the grey of lavender gloves and the snowy white flash on his rump. The so-called ringtails, hen birds or immature ones, are not unusual, but to see such a buccaneer in all his glory was an exciting experience. Lazily, he drifted over the field, a pause in his wingbeat, a glance from side to side with those fierce eyes, talons hanging just below his train. He made a playful, easy turn over one of my kestrels perched humbly on top of a dead willow, at which that hero dashed away in ignominious haste. The rakish buccaneer flew on, a spirit of the old fens of Hereward, and slipped out of sight across the lode dug by the Romans and with which, no doubt, his ancestors were familiar. My day was suddenly enriched by his passing.

Hawks and handsaws are two of our more desirable birds; both are flourishing in a quiet way and both are as easy to tell apart now as they were in Shakespeare's day.

Little brown ghost, 5 October 1995

Of all the quarry species, perhaps the woodcock is the one most revered by sportsmen – certainly by members of the **Shooting Times** *Woodcock Club. Here, in an article from 1995, John uncovers some of the bird's mystery.*

*'For fools are known by looking wise
As men find woodcocks by their eyes'*

H e comes in autumn following the ghosts of the Viking raiders across the North Sea. In he steals on a misty November night as silent as the prowling longships which his ancestors knew. There is no one out there in those dunes where the sea wind sighs so mournful to witness the end of his saga and the traveller dropping exhausted into the marram grass. Only the seals, the lonely gulls and the creatures of the night might see the speck lilting and drifting to sink down at journey's end.

Often he comes on the first full moon of the autumn, the woodcock moon, folk call it. To the ancients, anything touched by the moon was a potent talisman, for the silver disk swimming up the heavens was said to perturb men's minds and awaken the dark forces within us all. Ignorant of the miracle of migration, the old marsh dwellers must have wondered at the sudden arrival of this strange bird, dropping in under a cold moon, apparently from nowhere, or at best from a distant land of which they could have known nothing.

Sometimes he does not make it. A misjudgment of the weather and a sudden tempest from the West has him battling for his very life, close to the water, sometimes landing exhausted on the deck of a coaster or on a lighthouse. At others, weary to death, the steady wing beat slows then falters and, completely spent, he settles on the waves and succumbs. Wondering fishermen often haul him on board in their nets.

Those that arrive safely settle in the dunes and rest. They are dehydrated and tired and a smart lad may pick them up by hand, for birds of the year may never have seen another human being. They come with other migrants fleeing Scandinavian winter, clouds of chattering fieldfares and redwings having blazed the trail. With the woodcock comes the short-eared owl, that long-winged day hunter which wheels and soars over the marshes. The coincidence of its arrival gives it the old country name of woodcock owl.

The 'fall' of cock regains its strength and filters westwards, stacking up in Cornwall and West Wales and then spilling over into Ireland, that Mecca of woodcock shooters. In spring they drift back again, retracing their flight across the Norsemen's sea for nesting. Many remain here and nest in our own woods. Despite the westward migration they are found on the east coast throughout the season and, just when you least expect it, a cock is likely to spring from a rough corner of any shoot in the land. I have seen a woodcock high up on a grouse moor.

To describe the bird as being generally brown would be true, but would do it scant justice. How may one convey the bewildering array of every shade of brown which God created, from almost black to the palest shade of bleached grass? On his back, wings and breast you will find every tint of autumn in the woods, the dead leaves, faded reed, flaked bark and the fawn ditch bottoms choked with old rush he so loves.

Sometimes the Creator plays a harmless prank on woodcock lovers. He sends them one painted sooty black, another Isabelline, known to scientists as rufous leucistic, while a third might be as white as driven snow. Just now and then one will turn up with the usual plumage save for his primaries which are white. The Spaniards say that the three black stripes across his head are marks left by the fingers of the Blessed Virgin who, legend has it, took pity on the bird and gave it a long bill for probing the soft earth and made it the lonely prince of the moonlit corridors of the woodlands.

Even the length of his beak is likely to vary. Most are the standard 70mm or so but now and then there is one half as long. There are those, of whom I am not one, who become quite excited about this phenomenon. It has great soft eyes set high in its head the better to command all-round vision. The couplet by Butler which opens this piece refers to the fact that those who seek out cock will first see those great luminous orbs softly glowing against the backdrop of the forest floor.

That it carries its young between its thighs is indisputable. For 200 years naturalists and sportsmen of the highest repute have witnessed it and it remains only for some lucky and skilful soul to photograph it and the few die-hard doubting Thomases will be convinced. The mother will move her newly hatched young from the nest site to a place of soft mud for feeding. She grips the baby firmly between her thighs, tucks her long bill under her body supporting the chick beneath and flies heavily down to the edge of the stream. One by one she ferries the family to safety.

It is a taciturn bird but sometimes it croaks and at others whistles softly. Some refer to this whistle as roding while others believe roding to be the flight the bird makes down woodland rides at last light. Woodland stalkers will have seen it many times. Only a bounder would shoot woodcock roding or flighting out to feed. It is a sad testimony to the forefathers of our sport that Charles St John shot them from a deck chair in the evening, not only when they were roding but in summer when they had eggs and young.

I think it was Colin McKelvie, in his remarkable monologue *The Book of the Woodcock*, who said on a shooting day 'a pheasant is a pheasant, but a woodcock is an event'. There is an urge in many of us to shoot a woodcock at all costs. Many and many are the times that safety rules dinned into us and rigorously observed from childhood are flung to the winds in our lust for the prize. We must have it, that holiest of sporting Grails, now a safe, even easy shot in front but by the time you have it covered it is below the hedge line and directly in front of a stop or neighbouring Gun.

Having reached an age when insurance policies are maturing and self-preservation is suddenly important, I look round for a handy tree trunk when I hear the excited shriek "Cock forward!". There is the oldest of all woodcock stories, so famous that I hesitate to repeat it, in which an aged keeper attributed his longevity to the fact that he flung himself face down in the bracken the moment he heard that battle cry.

Everything about the bird is touched with magic. Its moonstone eyes, lonely wood nymph existence, its coming on the moon and even its flight all are fey. When first seen it flies straight enough so that it seems the veriest duffer could knock it down. In the blink of an eye it has dropped 5ft, flicked to the left then right, skimmed low over the headkeeper's hat, faded behind a frieze of willow twigs and is gone. Yet when one falls to the gun and the fierce thrill of elation courses through the veins, how many, I wonder, contemplate the broken body, the delicate bill scored by a pellet and that kaleidoscope of browns now muddied and bent without just a twinge of regret?

The Game Conservancy tells us that the bird is doing well enough and is in no danger, and even as I write Andrew Hoodless is conducting a survey into its strange ways. I wish him luck. How can anyone apply scientific research to a fairy?

For all the official reassurance there are some eminent estates stuffed with birds which have put a moratorium on woodcock. Are they, I wonder, taking what they deem to be a conservation measure, or are they succumbing to the subliminal guilt which makes us feel slightly uncomfortable when a line of woodcock is laid out with the bag at the end of the day?

Much is made, and rightly so, of the sporting feat of shooting a right-and-left at cock. The Bols Snippen Club, of fond memory, was adopted by *Shooting Times*. Anyone who makes the double shot in front of witnesses is entitled to a badge and the right to attend an annual dinner. I am a moderate shot and see few woodcock, but I have done it twice. There are those who have shot a hundred a year for half a lifetime and have never done it at all – more magic for you.

To those who marvel at such a shooting triumph, think on. The sculptor Chantrey shot two with one shot and brought them back to life in marble. His handiwork may be seen at Holkham Hall. If you think that is pretty good going reflect on the 23 Shots recorded by Gladstone who have killed two birds to their first barrel, many of them following it up with a third. Best of all was Lord Balfour in 1893 shooting in Scotland. Four woodcock rose at once and flew towards him. He shot them all with two barrels.

In an age of the common and universal knowledge of the Internet, the woodcock still holds a touch of mystery and some secret corners in its existence. Its habits, appearance, flight, secrecy, high tariff on the shooting man's scoresheet, its lunatic ways and waddling gait have become the cherry on the shooting cake, the pinch of salt which savours and something special on a day of run-of-the-mill pheasants. On the table with its trail intact – only a vandal would eviscerate one before cooking – it is the queen of the dining room.

Its pin feathers are prized trophies and you may fix them into the lower mandible the better to display them in your hatband. Frenchmen pour a measure of Cointreau down the throat of a freshly shot bird to flavour it. Gun engravers love to depict it on fine guns and woodcarvers dote on it. Elizabethans caught them in horsehair 'springes' and deemed them silly birds.

It is more than just a bird. It is a scrap of old wood magic, a rare and valued talisman, a creature which in an age of politicising and tedious experts still embodies something of the ancient spirit of the uncluttered and wild sport we all love.

The sentinel bird, **Country Life,** *2 February 2011*

The vigilant curlew will produce demented shrieking to warn fellow marsh dwellers of approaching fowlers but, as John wrote in his Countryman column in **Country Life** *in 2011, it is its haunting, lonely wail that makes it the most romantic of birds.*

> *'A curlew lean or a curlew fat,*
> *Carries twelve pence upon her back.'*

The largest of the 'hen footed fowl', the common curlew is also the most romantic, for it haunts the wildest and loneliest places, where its trembling, wailing cry sends a shiver down the spine. Its familiar double note mimics its name, and in spring it bubbles over with a sweetly trilling arpeggio of haunting melancholy like soft water cascading over pebbles. Its music stirred poets as diverse as Robbie Burns and Ted Hughes, not to mention Benjamin Britten and his *Curlew River.*

Some say the curlew is the spirit voice of drowned sailors, others say it is long-dead shepherds and, north of the border, where she is known as a whaup, she is considered a bird of ill omen; the Highlander classes her with witches, warlocks and 'things that go bump in the night', and Shetlanders regard with horror the very thought that anybody might want to eat one. A visitor who did just that was referred to afterwards in hushed tones as "the man that ate the whaup".

The curlew was once shot by wildfowlers and was good to eat if it had been feeding inland; a fat one might turn the scales at 3lb, making it attractive to a hungry longshoreman. The breast meat was plump, rich, dark and fibrous, just right for inclusion in the fowler's 'oystercock pie', into which went a variety of shore birds diverse enough to give an ornithologist a nervous breakdown.

There were two sorts of curlew, those that stayed on the tideline and ate marine life and others that preferred stubbles and high mosses. The latter were edible, the former distinctly kippery. Despite her desirability on a platter, fowlers often had cause to say unkind things about her, as, like the geese in ancient Rome, the curlew is a vigilant sentinel, warning other birds of the approach of the gunner. Together with redshank, she springs aloft with a series of shrieking cries, putting other birds on their guard when danger threatens. Many a big shot has been spoiled that way. In Yarrell's *British Birds* (fourth edition), we read of a curlew shrieking dementedly over the head of a sleeping seal and actually striking the animal with the tips of its wings to alert it, just as the hunter was raising his rifle.

For such a sagacious bird, the curlew can be called with ease. That liquid 'currrleeee currrleeee' whistle can be reproduced with practice and a little tonguing. A passing curlew is often suckered by it and will fly round the whistler many times, replying plaintively and peering down. Gunners of old used the trick to lure the bird within range; once, I got one to settle no more than a cricket pitch away in the field in which I stood.

Trying to catch one in a clap net for ringing is another matter. Assisting the late Dr Eric Ennion on the Northumbrian coast netting shore birds on the tideline, we caught several dunlin, ringed plover and others, but never a curlew, although sometimes they stalked and fed nearby, dwarfing the tiny stints and sandpipers. Like fowlers of old, we dreaded the appearance of the old whaup, for it was sure to spot us and give the game away.

Although the curlew, which has been protected since 1981, is not in immediate danger – there are an estimated 50,000 breeding pairs – she has suffered from upland drainage, predation and disturbance of nesting grounds by those exercising their right to roam.

All will know the curlew for her downward curving bill, so sensitive to the invertebrates that she tweezers from deep mud with such dexterity. Her mottled brown plumage is attractive in a muted way, and some of her wing feathers are sought by Cumbrian anglers for trout flies.

The common or Eurasian curlew is a strong and graceful flier with a charming and dainty spring display. Migrants arrive in the UK from the Continent when hard weather threatens. They fly in V- or wedge-shaped formations, their large size and distinctive beaks resembling so many ibises – the curlew is our very own rather dowdy ibis.

But it is always the voice, not the corporeal form, of the wandering spirit of the marshes that stirs us most. To hear it floating over a high moss or ringing along a misty foreshore as the tide flows on a lonely morning is to be stirred. The eerie call might be disturbing or uplifting, depending on your mood, but a heart of stone cannot fail but be moved by the sound.

The harvest mouse, Country Life, *10 August 2011*

John wasn't just one for the birds – in this article written for Country Life *in 2011, he introduces readers to Micromys minutes.*

> *'If e'er thy breast with freedom glowed*
> *And spurned a tyrant's chain,*
> *Let not thy strong oppressive force*
> *A freeborn mouse detain.'*
>
> *Barbauld, 1733*

The scythe was working well. More luck than skill with the stone had given the blade a keen edge and it swished through the dry Norfolk reed creating satisfying mayhem; a brown tide of my enemies swirled round my ankles. My sharpening stone hung dagger-like from the hip, and with long marsh boots and stout braces holding up corduroys, I was every inch a fen dyker.

Close enough to touch, swallows darted over the cut stems, snipping insects that drifted up, bewildered by the devastation of their world. The next downstroke was primed and loaded, but I paused, for in front of my nose, was a fist-sized nest woven into the stems. The season was advanced, the little home deserted, so I cut it out, stalks and all, as an exhibit for grandson's nature table. It was the nest of a harvest mouse.

Micromys minutus it is, and rarely does a Latin name so suit its holder. The harvest mouse is indeed extremely minutus, not to say micro, one of the smallest British mammals, weighing in dripping wet about the same as a 2p piece or a standard letter, half the size of a house mouse. It is an appealing little chap, generously endowed with the 'aah factor' with bush-baby eyes, large furry ears, quivering whiskers, dense brown fur and charming behaviour.

Most appealing is its prehensile tail. There is something irresistible about a harvest mouse with its tail curled round a stem, hanging on with its hind feet, whiskers trembling with endeavour as, with its forepaws, it wrestles into submission a tricky blackberry. It has toes made for climbing, as it spends its life twixt earth and heaven, halfway up thick hedges, reeds or cereals where ground predators rarely come. In winter, it ventures underground for brief periods for a short sleep, but doesn't favour long hibernation. Living for just 18 months, it's active day and night, cramming into a short life as much as it can, finding food, caring for its babies and nest-making.

Its nest is a wonder. No human fingers, however dextrous, could shred grass and weave the thin strips tightly round a fragile outer frame until it becomes firm. The mouse works from inside and out, threading the fibres back and forth through the mesh. This is done while clinging to swaying stalks with tail and hind feet, working with forepaws and teeth. The fact that she – to the female falls the responsibility for house construction – carries out this most intricate task at night adds to the incredible nature of the achievement. She doesn't rest after building one nest, but will make another, one for daily living and a larger one as a nursery.

The naturalist Gilbert White of Selbourne was brought a harvest-mouse nest. He believed the creature to be unknown to natural historians and that it was a new species. He remarked on the firmness of construction and observed that it was the size of a cricket ball, although, in 1769, the game was in its infancy and the ball was made of sheepskin. He found he could roll the nest along the table despite that fact that it contained eight pink harvest mouselets.

The young are born naked and blind, and a pair might produce up to seven litters in one year as, like all of their tribe, they are fecund. There is a current fashion for recycling old tennis balls with holes cut in them to be hung in hedges as faux harvest-mouse nests to encourage them to breed. The logic of this is questionable, although the sentiment admirable. If the mice are present, they have no trouble making their own nests. There is no evidence of the project enjoying success, although bumblebees occasionally adopt a Wimbledon reject as home.

The harvest mouse was so-called because it was most often seen in the harvest field, being fond of cereal stalks for nest-making, especially wheat and oats. Where they are common, some will seek out hedges and build nests about 3ft from the ground. The gentle old times of the sickle meant that when the corn was cut, a nest might be spared or lie undamaged in the sheaf until the occupants could make an orderly, nocturnal flit. Sometimes nest, parents and babies were bundled up by the reaper and taken to the barn or stack. What chance today with a combine harvester thundering through a field at running pace, where any nest and its occupants is snatched and pulverised in the blink of an eye? Modern agribusiness isn't kind to wildlife and has much for which to answer. It's a case of the meek not so much inheriting the earth as being ground into it.

The harvest mouse can be found across much of Europe, and in Britain it favours the south, rarely appearing north of Yorkshire. It hates the cold and wet. It is on the Red List as a low risk, although it grows scarcer; I wonder when any reader last saw one, although as they're retiring, it's possible to live close to them without knowing it. It eats small insects, grass seeds, berries and the cereals in which it nests. It has little defence strategy apart from self-effacement and is prey to owls, weasels, stoats, cats, hawks, crows and even pheasants. It is one of those creatures that everything likes to eat.

Minutus is charming, humble and utterly harmless. It will not come into houses like its cousins and is a threat to nothing, doing harm to nobody. In other words, it possesses all the qualities for being sidelined, a candidate for elimination in the thrusting world of the 21st century – tennis balls notwithstanding.

Wild thing, 27 April 2000

Taking creatures from the wild may be frowned upon today, but as this article from 2000 illustrates, a close study of various birds at an early age cemented John's love of nature.

For centuries, man has taken and tamed birds of prey to help him with his hunting. By using a wide range of ancient skills he has harnessed the awesome killing powers of these most neurotic of birds, either to fill his cooking pot or to provide sport for his master.

The Victorian bird-catchers set their fine nets and limed twigs to take goldfinches and linnets for collectors. The birds were kept as pets or more often, used in singing competitions in London pubs. Great sums would change hands as each bird in turn sang its heart out in those smoky hellholes, pining, no doubt, for the woods and thistle fields they once knew. Many others kept such birds as diversions and poor Victorians might even have kept one hanging in its cage in the parlour.

'I walked behind with my old cock linnet' is a line from a popular music-hall song and no more than a reflection of common practice instantly recognisable by the audience. Even when it was made illegal, the trade went on into the 1930s. The catchers would keep their victims in a paper bag, so that if the law came along, the bag could easily be torn open and the evidence essential for a conviction could escape.

As with these singing finches and hunting raptors, man has always had a weakness for taming and keeping wild creatures. It seems, perhaps, that this was one way of having a slice of nature tamed and at your disposal, bringing a scrap of the countryside into grimy lives and, in the absence of TV and radio, having a voice in the house apart from your own. The parrot was universally popular for its intriguing ways, longevity, ease with which it adapted to captivity, and the huge advantage that it could be taught to mimic human speech.

The poor man's parrot for years was either a jackdaw or a magpie, both of which, being corvids, are easily tamed, intelligent, and responsive to human company. Several lads in the fen village of my childhood had a tame jackdaw, for magpies were still uncommon then.

The beauty of such a bird was that it did not need to be kept in a cage but could fly free and drop in for some human company when it felt like it.

Much later, in my teaching days, a boy brought his jackdaw to school. It caused some excitement as it flew around, calling hoarsely, disturbing lessons, and its owner could claim blissfully that it was a wild bird out of his control and not his fault. It took to attacking the cross-country team running round the silage in white singlets, so that its owner was ordered to capture it and take it home on the bus.

A lady in my village also kept a magpie. It had been found, abandoned by her son, and responded well to tender, loving care and three square meals a day. It flew freely round the house and perched on the pictures, uttering raucous cries. It was a handsome beast decked out in black and white, with a metallic sheen and a bright eye.

One day, it sat on the shoulder of the lady of the house and, without warning, darted its dagger beak into her eye. It had been attracted by the glint, a weakness all corvids have for bright things – it was the undoing, you will recall, of the ill-fated Jackdaw of Rheims, which stole the Bishop's ring and fell on hard times as a result.

The eye was undamaged but bruised, and that was the end of the magpie. They felt it might do the same to an unsuspecting child, with more serious results. The tales of long-lost wedding rings and other jewellery found in jackdaw's nests are as legion as they are apoctyphal – it was a favourite literary ruse of Victorian dramatists. The missing will found in the fabric of the a crow's nest was an unfailingly successful last-page resolution of the most opaque mysteries.

It was said that you could teach a jackdaw to speak but to do so, you had to split its tongue with a silver sixpence. This nonsense had its roots in old-fashioned witchcraft and was as cruel as it was unnecessary. The only word I ever heard any jackdaw utter was 'Jack'.

However, all corvids were thought to be birds of darkness, scavengers after ancient battles, lamb-killers, and familiars of wise women and witches. Tales of them are steeped in old lore, sinister legend and horror stories, indeed, writer Edgar Allen Poe chose the raven as the subject of one of his best black tales.

The old country vicarage in which I was raised had a tenement of a rookery, in the elms round the lawn by the church. The trees and rooks have long gone, but they were a source of continual childhood delight and sowed the seeds of a love of birds. Every May, there seemed to be a gale and a clutch of scrofulous orphans of the stone would be blown from their nests and sit glumly in the nettles cawing plaintively.

My mother would rescue them and set up an emergency field dressing-station in the wash house, feeding them on bread and milk. This was quite the wrong diet, but the argument ran that such fare was good for children so it must be good for rooks. In no time, they became imprinted on her and she could not walk down the garden to cut a cabbage or hang out the washing without being followed by a suppliant army of young rooks, which flapped along behind her, cawing imploringly to be fed. In time, many of them grew strong enough on the wing to return to the treetops whence they came.

Much later, I took on a tawny owl which had flown into some tennis netting and been damaged. He lived in a roomy ferret hutch in the garden and I fed him on mice and day-old chicks – all raptors must have bone, fur and feather in their diet to allow their innards to work and for them to eject the pellet of compacted indigestibles. Other owls would come at night and talk to him through the wire. Maybe they were working out an escape plan but, before it could happen, events moved on. A student at my school was mad keen to have the owl and I promised he could, on condition he made a suitable aviary. He went to town and built a large wire structure full of hollow logs, dense greenery, and a nesting box. He had even incorporated a 'real' tree in the middle.

I grabbed Old Owly, as he was known, put him in a cardboard box and took him to his new home. I heard later that the lad took the box inside, opened it carefully and Old Owly shot out, straight through the aviary door which he had left open. This audacious dash for freedom meant that the owl never enjoyed its new home, but sat about on the trees at night and kept the family awake with its hooting. No doubt it lives to this day none the worse for its adventure.

The conclusion is that wild creatures do not make good pets and rarely live in captivity for long, They are best left alone, no matter how lost they may appear. The mother knows pretty well where the 'lost' infant is concealed and will care for it. Children coming in with 'lost' young blackbirds should be sent straight back to return them to where they found them. They rarely live in captivity for long.

As for those well-meaning ignoramuses we see reported in the local paper as having 'rescued' leverets found in a field, they spend months feeding the creatures with an eye dropper and all too often they die. When they do survive, what do you do with an imprinted hare when an adult? There have been famous cases of tame hares becoming good pets, but they are outnumbered a hundred to one by those stories which end in tears.

Charles St John told of a tame roebuck which was taken as a fawn and kept in a pen. Its fear of humans turned to aggression, so its keeper did not dare enter the run without arming himself with a stout wooden shield to repel its charges. One tame roebuck killed a boy sent to feed it.

My friend Jack has a golden eagle named Max – Mad Max would be more appropriate. He was used to hunt hares and he was spectacular to see in action. But, his instincts also turned to aggression and he became such a handful, attacking passers-by and innocent bystanders, that he is now confined to barracks. He must by now be all of 30 years old.

The answer is not to take and attempt to keep wild birds or animals at home. Rarely does it work, you are taking on a major commitment which might last for some years, while returning tame creatures to the wild once they have become imprinted is very difficult. Having said as much, there are few things that cannot be tamed and kept with expert loving care. Foxes, rabbits, songbirds, raptors, owls, deer, badgers and many others have been tried with mixed success. The notable exception is the wild cat that is untameable. Take an unweaned kitten with its eyes shut and it will still hate you, no matter how kind to it you are.

Apart from legal considerations that outlaw the taking of most birds, for amateurs with the best of intentions it is rarely successful, and the birds are best left to fend for themselves and take whatever nature has in store.

If you must keep something at home, then make it a goldfish, a budgerigar or a dog, but even then you will be taking on a long commitment and probably many tears. I urge you to steer clear of cats in every circumstance, but you don't need me to tell you that.

Chasing the birds, 12 June 2003

Armed with anoraks and binos, in 2003 John and his good friend the sporting artist Will Garfit indulged in a spot of shameless twitching. In doing so they proved the point that you cannot be a true shooter without having a wider interest in natural history.

We had the binoculars, the telescope, shapeless woolly jumpers, big boots and RSPB checklist, but drew the line at the bobble hat and anorak. My old mate Will Garfit and I were to steal 24 hours from glorious May and become twitchers for a day. Will had read my list of garden birds recorded one morning and decided that we ought to do the job properly and see how many we could bag in a day on the delectable north Norfolk coast. What's more, we were not going to shoot any of them, the pointing finger was to be more powerful than the smoking gun. Stopping at Humphreys Towers long enough to share an enormous trout and pyramid of home-grown asparagus with rivulets of melted butter, we set off northwards as a golden sun sank over a green landscape polka-dotted with blossom.

We decided to start straight away, and as Will drove we called out sightings and I ticked them on the list. Grey partridge was a good one, for they are scarce and the corn was tall enough to hide them. Arriving at dusk, we crept through bosky thickets and gorse clumps overlooking the crawling sea where we bagged a grand right-and-left. At the same time we heard a nightjar 'churring' and the soul-stirring music of a nightingale. We stumbled on a courting couple, but they did not count. When dusk slipped into darkness we dropped into the Salthouse pub for a couple of stiffeners before turning in ready for an early start the following day.

At 5am we were on the Cley Marshes, excellently run by the Norfolk Naturalists Trust, walking down the winding boardwalk with a wall of Norfolk reed on either side and into the thatched hide. On the way we scored a bearded tit, reed warbler and sedge warbler, while far away a lordly marsh harrier circled on shallow-angled wings.

The hide was in darkness, but on opening one of the observation shutters the room was bathed in soft light. A window had opened on a fairyland of lovely birds. When I was a small boy an avocet was as rare as a roc, with only one or two breeding on the Halvergate marshes. Here, they were common, wading daintily in the shallows, delicate upturned bills sweeping for crustaceans. Then, in quick succession, it was dunlin, ruff, black-tailed godwit, wigeon, mallard, teal, shelduck, oystercatcher, redshank, peewit, grey plover, common tern, pied wagtail – thick and fast they came and my hand was a blur keeping the checklist up to date. We were voyeurs, seeing all while remaining unseen. From the distant dunes arrowed a male hobby, the handsome little falcon flying ten yards over our heads, feather perfect in the morning sun.

We twitchers do not hang about and we dashed off to explore a scrap of woodland that rang with the song of warblers. Whitethroat, chiffchaff, blackcap and another nightingale, a russet smudge in the thicket singing his heart out along with an assortment of finches, tits and other woodland birds. Already the list looked impressive but my stomach was screaming for breakfast. This birding is hungry work. A whole pound of bacon, half-a-dozen eggs and six rounds of toast later we were ready for more action. A short-eared owl drifted over the reeds, a heron stalked in a pool while greylags cackled and gabbled, flying in pairs and settling on the close cropped grazing marshes.

A raiding party to the cliffs at Old Hunstanton gave us fulmar, turnstone and various gulls, and then we dropped into the RSPB reserve at Titchwell. This was a star, for we moved from woodland to fresh water, on to brackish and finally to the coast, scoring new 'hits' all the way. We saw ruddy duck; no doubt the owners will be down some time to shoot them. The star attraction was a black-winged stilt stalking on impossibly long, sealing-wax red legs. A personal triumph was a garganey that I picked up with Will's telescope. Will birds as he shoots, lightning fast, with complete certainty and a deal quicker than I. On the shore we scooped brent goose, sanderling, cormorant, bar-tailed godwit and eider duck before we flitted a mile further for a leg-numbing trudge through the soft sand of the dunes.

This was less productive, but we picked up meadow pipit, swift, swallow and yellowhammer. We sat down to glass the tideline, some little terns passed and my eyelids felt suddenly heavy. I was about to nod off when Will hauled me to my feet. This was not the place for a rest, he knew a better spot half a mile off. So at last we lounged in spiky grass gazing at the marsh, having taken in little egret, whimbrel, and curlew, and got stuck into a huge pork pie from the shop, apples, tomatoes and some chocolate. Put that lot inside a middle-aged man who has been up since 5am and walked some distance in the sun and he becomes a flower nodding on its stalk at noon. Soon the sound of gentle snoring competed with the clamouring gulls.

Two dogs belonging to walkers spied our lifeless bodies in the grass and woke us with a volley of barking. Ask a fowler where he shot that bag of wigeon and he grows evasive, as silent as a frog full of shot. The birders were the opposite, sharing sightings with us, pointing out the spotted redshank that we would have missed and inviting me to look through their telescope.

Refreshed, we set off down a coastal track thinking that we had seen most of it, for our list was pretty full. In a meadow this side of the sea wall, Will snapped up a quick trio of golden plover, wheatear and reed bunting. The sun slid down the sky putting the marshes into soft focus, tipping every reed blade with copper. At dusk, at Will's cottage in Cley, we were about to count the bag when there was a spotted flycatcher sitting on the wire. We had not seen woodpeckers, barn owl, bittern, mistle thrush or other birds we might have expected, but for all that had bagged an amazing 101 species with two possibles not included.

The good fowler should know his birds and it does no harm to spend a day like that now and then. Like a couple of magpies we chattered all the way home, but kept a sharp eye out of the window for a barn owl. We serious twitchers never let up.

Rookincarnation, 18 May 2006

After a close call, medically speaking, John was in a reflective mood in May 2006. As his Country Gun column shows, life in a rookery has a certain attraction.

Assuming there is such a thing as reincarnation, you might pass an idle moment after a life-threatening heart attack wondering what creature you would like to return as. Most options have a downside. For a while I fancied coming back as a pinkfoot goose, but all those cold nights sitting on mudflats and the ever-present risk that a local wildfowler might fill you full of buckshot dulled the gloss of anserine life. A return as a British black panther might do, for, being mythical, you would be indestructible. Otter? Liable to wandering into fox snares and hated by anglers. Badger? Enemy of cattle farmers and often run over on the road. Wasp? Likely to be sprayed or have its nest nuked by the pest man. Garden bird? Prey to sparrowhawks and cats. Sparrowhawk? All things at the top of the food chain lead risky lives. Cat? Do me a favour...

So what was it to be? After long thought, I came up with the answer – a rook. Nobody really shoots rooks any more since rook pie dropped off the menu in Egon Ronay eateries. You are never lonely and have a cheerful gang of noisy mates. There is no shortage of food and you are not a fussy trencherman; you enjoy life, relish daredevil flying and love a good natter. You live long enough to learn a few things, but not so long that it becomes boring and, for a bird, you have more than your share of brains. Nothing much attacks you, though you have to keep an eye cocked for a passing peregrine. No fox can get at you and nowadays not even small boys steal your eggs. You are a master house builder and make a sturdy dwelling in a tenement in the topmost twigs, where you look down on the world in safety and lofty dominance of all you survey.

You are a loving and monogamous spouse, taking responsibility for your noisy children, keeping them fed and protected. Whether you establish your colony on a roundabout, on a motorway or in a country churchyard, you enjoy being around humankind. Loyal to a nesting site that you will not desert for a century, you can predict the approaching death of the householder upon which your whole tribe makes clamorous, raucous flight. You can tell when a tree is sick from a lessening pliancy of the topmost twigs. Equally useful is that, without even trying, you beat Michael Fish and his tribe at weather forecasting, and when storms come, you ride them out and relish being buffeted high and tossed wildly across the heavens. Yes indeed, there are worse things you could return as than a rook.

Mid-May I turn my mind to the sable birds of the shining furrows and, unlike last year when they mysteriously vanished, the colony down the footpath seems to have had a trouble-free nesting season. I love their cheeky antics, eavesdrop on their conversations, watch their parliaments, enjoy their agility on the wing and admire the way the community rubs along, neighbour getting on harmoniously with neighbour. How favourably that picture of easygoing tolerance compares with human housing estates. My *Shooting Times* colleague, Petrel, sings rooks' praises and I join in the chorus.

My young life was closely bound to them, for there was a rookery outside my bedroom window and I watched them for many an hour. At about this time of year the squire came round with his pals and with whipcrack rifles and booming shotguns shot the branchers, the scrofulous squabs plummeting down into the cow parsley. I peered fearfully over the window ledge, clutching a tear-stained handkerchief, for these were my friends (I mean the birds, not the squire), and at such sorrowful moments I could never see myself becoming a shooting man.

I used to eat rook pie but it was not much cop and was only a way of using up good protein when we let nothing go to waste. Now, we do not need rook pie with a Tesco up the road. Rooks mostly eat farm pests and woe betide the day they vanish from the land.

Miserable people will write of rooks killing lambs, digging up corn and stealing partridge eggs. Such people miss the big picture, for odd rogues do not condemn a whole species or where would humankind be?

A message to you few corvicides still living in the dark ages. Next time you think of taking aim at a passing rook, pause a moment and reflect that it just might be poor old Country Gun reincarnated that you have in you sights, so either lower your gun or aim very true indeed.

The goddess of the field, 7 March 2012

No beast of the field could compete with the hare, a creature steeped in magic and mythology – and good to eat, too.

'A hopper of ditches,
a cropper of corn,
A wee brown cow with a pair
of leather horns.'

As a youth, I always took a chance at a hare as it burst from its form in the stubble or potatoes and went streaking away. The sexton's old hammergun flew to the shoulder with the confidence of youth and more often than not, puss would roll over in a blur of flailing legs and blown fleck. If outward bound, I could hang her in the shade of an elder bush where flies do not go, to be collected on the homeward journey. Otherwise she had to be carried in the net-fronted gamebag or slung across the shoulder in the old manner in a rope noose, but being young and strong that was no hardship. My father would do the skinning and my mother the cooking, for jugged hare was popular in our house in those meat-starved post-war years.

Reuben the Norfolk farmer lay a-dying but, at 92 years old, he was ready to meet his maker. His family clustered round to catch his final words, a gem of wisdom gleaned from almost a century on the land. His sons bent low hearkening to the thin breathing; might even now the old boy tell of a new will or some unguessed at hidden treasure? Summoning his strength the old fellow lifted his head and drew a rasping breath. The listeners cocked their ears and leaned close. "Allus look an oat stubble for a heer…" he gasped, and expired. It was his most valuable secret.

Hares are curious and magical beasts upon which medieval venery bestowed many names: the swift as wind; the skulker; the animal that dwells in the corn; the white-bellied one, and so on. She is sister of the cold moon and familiar of the hearth; in China one does not say 'The

Man in the Moon', but 'The Hare in the Moon'. She was said to be male and female at the same time, is a ruminant that grazes but chews no cud, eating her food twice by gnawing half-digested pellets of dung. Unique among beasts she seeks no shelter but lies out on open land in a scrape or form. Many a farm boy has spotted her thus and fired a shot but she scampers off unscathed, that cunning earthwork protected her vitals. She deposits her young here and there on the eggs-in-one-basket principle, suckling them at night; a timorous beast she will see off a fox that threatens her leveret.

She runs away uphill, never down. She can see behind her but not very well ahead. She never walks but hops, making her look ungainly but, when fleeing, her powerful back legs send her streaking away. Sometimes she runs for pure joy, for hares used to race taxiing planes on a grass airfield in Ireland, lining up like sprinters ready for the off. She can swim the wide dykes of the saltings and leap like a salmon; one cleared an 8ft wall. She can be started in woodland and in March dances and boxes on the windy heaths until the fur or fleck drifts on the wind. A group of hares is known as a huske.

She was familiar to witches. Many a crone was cruelly treated in the dark days because cottagers believed she turned into a hare under the full moon and caused cattle to abort or fall sick. Anyone knows that it takes a silver bullet to kill her. A hare or cat oft was buried under churches and houses to ward off evil spirits. Queen Boudicca released one from the folds of her cloak on the day of battle to show her army which way to go. A hare foot in your pocket brought good fortune and was also used by goldsmiths to sweep up gold dust from their workbenches.

According to T.H. White (author of *The Once and Future King*), she was the favourite quarry of Master William Twyti, huntsman of Uther Pendragon. He talked calmly of great boars and stags and showed you his scars, but mention a hare and he would thump his glass on the table and discourse on this amazing animal declaring that, 'you could never blow a menee for her because the same hare could at one time be male and another female while it carries grease and croteyed and gnawed which things no beast on earth did except it.' Hares may be decoyed with a hare pipe or by mouth, vied the noted Lincolnshire poacher

Mackenzie Thorpe. Many and cunning were the 'engines' and subterfuges designed by ploughboys to catch her, for she was a great prize in a poor man's pot. A choice turnip left in a field, or parsley seed secretly sown on a stubble drew her like a nail to a magnet.

She had her favourite tracks, so nets could be strung across gates or snares set in smeuses and a broken coated lurcher sent to start her. Sometimes old-fashioned deception was enough. Spot a hare in the form and, avoiding eye contact, walk round her drawing ever closer until you can throw a coat over her. When the squires sat on the Bench enforcing the Game Laws they themselves had enacted, a poor man might be sent to the colonies for seven years for less.

The mass slaughter of hare shoots has declined. They accounted for hundreds of hares in one day in a free-for-all massacre of the innocents organised by farmers worried for their crops. The heavy shot aimed by inexperienced farm boys pecks at the fur as poor puss wails like a spanked child and escapes swinging a broken back leg. For reasons unknown, her population now is patchy, some places having none and others showing signs of revival. Warm summers are kind to her. Few shoots permit puss (or Sally or Old Sarah) to be fired at as she streaks through the line, a rule more for safety than conservation. Many a peppered gaiter may be credited to her deceptive speed.

She remains legal quarry, though coursing her with greyhounds is outlawed and the scourge of illegal coursing has declined. Shoot her if she is close enough, for she is good to eat if carefully prepared though some modern palates find her flesh too strong. As you take aim, reflect that you are shooting at a visitor from the frozen moon, one who capers crazily in its beams, confidant of witches, goddess of ancient peoples, favourite of Dark Age huntsmen, environmental barometer of the health of the land, the cat who lurks in the broom, the starer with wide eyes, spirit of the hearth, one who saw a Roman army defeated, was responsible for sending good men to Van Diemen's Land, companion of, and defender from, evil spirits who could be shot only with a silver weskit button.

I lost my enthusiasm for hare shooting in middle age; I ate one a year and was happy to shoot her for the pot, but she carried too much baggage. The organised hare shoot became shameful to me, but now people on bird shoots tend to leave her alone as much because of the no ground game rule as anything, a rule that implies that the modern Shot is not to be trusted with anything not up in the sky. I prefer those shoots that say you may shoot a hare if you are sure you can kill it and on you will take it home and eat it. A sportsman happy to have the blood of such a marvel on his hands had better aim true and be quite sure he is prepared for the consequences. It does not do to upset a witch...

Trees for pheasants, 3 November 2010

The key principles of siting woodland and hedges need to be considered to make the most of the birds on your shoot and, in this practical article from 2010, John explains how today's shooters can leave a fantastic legacy in so doing.

Men plant trees that their sons may sit in the shade – a pretty concept and, thanks to generations long dead, we enjoy a landscape laid out by sporting squires a century ago as harbourage for their game and foxes – as well as enjoying the shade on a sunny day.

A pheasant is a bird of the borders; it likes the edges of spinneys and rides, but is not so happy deep in the heart of dense forests. He who plants woodland for pheasants must remember the four guidelines: he is looking to provide shelter from the wind, breeding sites for nesting birds, holding cover and the facility to make the birds fly high on a shooting day.

Around the outside of the wood should be a hedge comprising double rows of whitethorn, blackthorn, a few firs, lonicera and laurel. The hedge should be a tractor-width from the edge of the wood to provide shelter. A tractor may drive round and cut it and it does not grow tall enough to impede farm machinery or shade, nor should it take nutrients from the field beyond. The hedge should be kept short and thick, and not allowed to grow tall and straggly. The treeless strip between wood and hedge is a good nesting place, a trapping site and even a spot for a small release pen.

The main covert should include larch, for this is a popular roosting tree, warm and dense enough, and impenetrable to the prying eyes of poachers at night. The important point is that your trees are not destined to become monarchs of the forest a century later, towering high above the surroundings and visible by satellite.

Trees such as beeches may look fine enough, but they make a dense canopy of leaves through which daylight cannot penetrate, so none of the vital ground cover can grow and the winter wind whistles between the trunks. A 30ft-high tree is tall enough.

Avoid conifers in solid blocks, for they are competitive and suppress all life below them. Also, they become impenetrable for beaters and too thick for pheasants, of use only for roosting. Nowadays, such lumps of forestry have rides cut for access and firebreaks that the shoot manager may use, while the modern trend is to mix the conifers with clumps of deciduous softwoods to relieve the tedium of endless firs.

Bear in mind the shooting day and the manner in which the trees will affect it. Place the Guns on a narrow ride and they will have no time even to snap-shoot birds flashing across the gap. Drive your birds from woodland that is too dense and they will struggle up, consuming huge amounts of energy corkscrewing to treetop height and setting off half-heartedly, only to glide down to land a short way off.

It is best to move the birds gently towards the edge of the woodland, where there is low cover, bushes, sewelling or brash with nettles or willow herb growing through it, a flushing point. The trick is to have a holding/flushing area, then a graduated series of shrubs, each higher than the last, over which the birds will rise gradually. The pheasants will fly over rather than through this cover, thus presenting good shots when they reach the Guns. This flushing point should be about 50 yards from the edge of the wood.

The wood proper should comprise about 60 per cent softwood and 40 per cent hardwood. A chessboard pattern of hardwood groups in a softwood forest is better than ordinary line planting. Whitebeam, crab apple, willow, scrub oak, cherry, hazel, snowberry, mountain ash, laurel and the excellent wild privet – which will keep warmth in on the coldest days – as well as larch and spruce make a reasonable combination and will not grow too tall to kill the ground cover. Such trees may easily be thinned or pollarded when necessary, for it is sometimes forgotten in the enthusiasm of first planting how quickly trees grow and how soon those you thought you had planted miles apart from each other are touching.

Siting the wood is important, assuming that you are in the fortunate position of being able to pick and choose. You can experiment with covercrops for a year or two, finding favoured areas and flight patterns and prevailing wind – bear in mind that you want to fly your birds between 200 yards and 500 yards. Ideally, you will plant trees on a slightly elevated site, so that Guns may be stood below it. Beware hilltops, as they are tempting sites, but they cannot be warmed up and the birds do not like them. You can plant a small spinney on high ground linked by a belt to the main wood, which may be much lower or even in a hollow and thus no good for showing birds. The main wood may be driven out along the strip and into the top one, from which birds may be flown in a spectacular way. The skill of the headbeater and his team is essential to making all this work and ensuring that game is neither walked over nor flushed too soon, nor in the wrong place. Dogs are not advised in the best beating lines in woods, unless they are exceptionally well trained.

It is unusual for anyone to take on a treeless shoot and, usually, there are established shelter belts, often completely degraded and almost useless. As well as planting new woodland, old woods can be restored if a team of shoot helpers takes a bit at a time, clearing dead wood and planting clumps of quick-growing ground cover, such as snowberry, bramble or willow for pollarding and a few firs.

It might be necessary in all new plantings to protect young trees against deer and rabbits. Fencing is expensive, so culling might help, as well as the provision of fraying stocks, which are willow stubs on which deer can thrash their antlers. Do not forget the most important thing – the perimeter hedge that makes all the difference. Ideally, the flushing end of the wood should come to a slight point to concentrate the birds at a spot from which they may spread out when flushed and to make them less likely to fly back over the wood. It is best to fly birds down sun rather than into it.

Large, old woods are not very good for showing birds, as pheasants are easily walked over and are reluctant to leave the wood and fly over open ground. Here, use a covercrop next to the wood, placed a field or so away. This may be driven away from the wood and the birds will fly back over the beaters' heads to Guns lined out on the wood side. Rides may be cut or enhanced and the wood driven in blocks, but birds can leak out of the sides of drives. A pheasant wood of no more than six acres can show good sport and hold a surprising amount of game. The big wood may look promising, but the pheasant is a bird of the boundaries and a big wood has only one.

Thus, your new woodland will enhance the countryside, your children will sit in the shade and your gamebirds will feel warm, safe and fly excitingly from it. How much better to plant your own wood and name it than to drill blocks of covercrops of maize and other non-native species?

The Britain we know and love, featured on 1,000 calendars and preserved on magazine covers, is the one laid down by Edwardian landowners and foresters who knew their business. It may fairly be said that the cherished landscape of this fair country has been shaped by the pheasant and the fox.

The bird band riffing the forest rides, 24 March 2010

Two worlds collide in this article from **Country Life** *– John's love of jazz and his love of nature unite as the woodpigeon plays sousaphone, the wren the piccolo and the song thrush soars as Louis Armstrong. The dawn chorus is the natural world's version of a New Orleans jazz band.*

Having spent a fragment of a well-spent life playing trumpet in a band on Bourbon Street, New Orleans, the sound of a distant parade sets my hair crackling. The late Sir John Dankworth did much to bridge the rift between jazz and classical. He said, "Beware purists; they mess everything up." Louis Armstrong growled in his gravely voice, "There's two sorts of music, man, good and bad." Thus to the dawn chorus, to which I hearken as I might a marching band many streets away, parading in old New Orleans on a sweltering afternoon. The lower-register instruments sound first, the pumping sousaphone and bass drum, and one by one the others fade in until, rounding the bend, you get the lot in full-blast stereo, each instrument individual, everyone ad-libbing, but the effect a harmonious whole.

Like the marching band, the dawn chorus is a free show and, to hear it, choose a fine morning in late April or early May. Close to London, Epping Forest becomes a concert hall for one of the greatest musicals in Britain. Wrap up warmly, take a folding chair and a flask of coffee, sit back, close your eyes and enjoy. Arrive in the pre-dawn hush, for some members of our band are early risers, and a lucky fan might catch the sweet trilling of the grasshopper warbler, nightingale or wood warbler warming up in the dark.

Standing on South Rampart Street, you half hear a distant sound: yes, there it is again, coming and going. You stop, cock your head and close your eyes. It's the rhythmical bump of the sousaphone, that serpentine piece of musical plumbing invented, as a jazz wag told me, by the famous brass band composer John Phillip Phone. Back in the forest, it is the basso cooing of a woodpigeon, backed by the breathy trombone of a tawny owl sounding like a cow blowing across the top of a milk churn. The bass line laid down, there is an explosive burst of piccolo from a wren. For one of our smallest birds, its chirrups, whistles and trills are deafening at close range.

The clarinet fades in – George Lewis, perhaps, or Johnny Dodds – in the shape of a blackbird, shouting the odds from a beech, staking claim to his territory, his mellifluous carolling making the woodland ring. He is one of the first to sing, unlike the song thrush, whose sweeter, more edgy song is preferred by many. She is a slugabed, however, not joining until the band has warmed up, although she sings later in the evening when the blackbird has put his instrument in its case.

There comes a roll on the snare drum; a great spotted woodpecker hammers on a dead ash, a staccato machine-gun rattle. Then his cousin, the green woodpecker – or yaffle – swoops across the ride in undulating flight with a burst of maniacal laughter. These are minor punctuation marks on the score, irrelevant contributions from over-enthusiastic spectators on the sidewalk, for one by one the serious musicians join in.

The robin is in full song now, unlike his fitful half-choruses of autumn and winter; he, too, is informing anyone with ears to hear that this is his patch and, Christmas card bird or not, he knows how to scrap to defend it. Britain's smallest bird, the goldcrest, has enjoyed a return, and you might hear his reedy treble weaving among the notes of his greater brethren. The blackcap pipes, a jay blows his harsh kazoo, a chaffinch rings his tubular bell and, at last, the song thrush strikes up, the Louis Armstrong and leader of the band – soaring arpeggios, exuberant riffs and repeated phrases, 'lest you think he never can recapture the first fine careless rapture.' He outplays the blackbird as in one of the cutting contests of the old jazzers when each tried to outdo the other, notes like icicles ringing along the balconies of the French Quarter.

Hard to miss the ocarina of the cuckoo, as he should be here by now, although his numbers shrink every year – what a loss if he failed to arrive at all. What is summer without a cuckoo and a swallow?

Some band members grow as frail as those in Preservation Hall. Farmland birds – such as yellow hammer, willow warbler and corn bunting – decline, and the 'croo croo' of the turtle dove is rare, its eggs preyed upon by our plague of magpies, squabs picked off by sparrowhawks. Ancient chroniclers told us all was well as long as 'the voice of the turtle is heard in the land.' Its diminution bodes ill.

If the song thrush is Armstrong, the nightingale is Bix Biederbecke, that sublime cornet player who died in his twenties before his genius had fully flowered. Like him, the nightingale is endangered, as muntjac have browsed the scrub that it and the willow warbler love. Bend down and you can peer from end to end of the wood, so degraded is the forest floor.

We round the bend and there is the band in full flow – in front, the leader capering with his decorated parasol just as a little egret, one of our newer birds, flies silent overhead. Some we lose, but we gain collared doves, once rare vagrants, now in every suburban garden, and egrets are here to stay, with Egyptian geese, cranes, goshawks and other European travellers moving north as – so we are told – climate change begins to bite.

Turn and watch as the band passes, amateur instrumentalists joining in, children dancing and all the infectious excitement that only New Orleans can engender. The parade passes, turns left into Basin Street, the music fades, one by one the instruments drift off, until at the end, you catch the last grunts of the sousa as it also dies away. Rise stiffly from your chair – it is full daylight. Take your empty flask and, with the band silent, save for the last woodpigeon cooing softly, uplifted and purged, make your way back to the madness of the real world.

On the Hook

Asking John to live with shooting at the expense of fishing would be like asking him which arm he'd prefer to have removed. Although he was best associated with shooting, the urge to cast a fly had a similar grip on him – it was a passion he shared with his sons, as a number of the articles represented in this section show.

Grafham Storm, 2 July 1981

In one of his earlier fishing articles, from 1981, John recounts the story of an extraordinary day on Grafham Water.

I t was high summer before I could find the time to fish Grafham Water, which is one of my favourite stillwater fisheries. Since it opened in 1967, the banks have grown green, trees matured and birds proliferated so that now it seems that the huge lake was made by Nature and not by Man. After 14 years devoted to fishing, sailing and birdwatching, each of superb quality, there are ominous rumblings about the future. In common with smaller concerns, the Anglian Water Authority is anxious to obtain the highest financial return from its amenities and there is talk of power-boats, water-skis, caravans and other brash and intrusive pursuits which, while undoubtedly profitable, would make uncomfortable bedfellows for the tranquil pursuits already established.

A proposal was even made to let the fishing, in its entirety, to the highest bidder – a matter which at the time of writing, remains unresolved. The retirement of the popular and admirable David Fleming Jones as fishery manager seems to have left some aspects, such as the administration of the trout fishing, in a less than satisfactory state, although the sport has remained excellent.

However, such worries are easily forgotten when one is out with a pal, bobbing up and down in a boat, lulled by the slap slap of the wavelets on the hull. The bailiffs, cheery as ever, had pushed us off from the jetty and wished us luck and now we had each other's company, a vast bag of food and quantities of fishing tackle with which to while away a long, summer day. Cuckoos and turtle-doves called and answered across the water, mallard duck-lings, distinguishable from their parents only by their fluffier feathers, for they were the same size, furrowed the water as they chased the midges.

It was, for once, a perfect morning with no excuse for failure. It soon became obvious that fish were feeding on chironomids just below the surface. Humping rises, slight bulges and tiny dimples could, by close observation, just be detected. To induce a take it was necessary to cast very accurately, to put the fly right on the nose of a feeding fish. If it fell only a few inches short, or if it overshot, the fish did not seem prepared to divert to take it. The reason was obvious. The warm, upper layers of water were full of nymphs, snails, caenis, hatching sedges, midge pupae – in fact, everything the trout gourmet desires.

The breeze died away leaving us in that state of waterborne immobility which would have been familiar to the Ancient Mariner. A tiny dimple broke the surface 15 yards ahead; the break was so small that it could have been made only by the smallest of stockfish. For the lack of any other presentable target, I covered it. "Look at that!" I exclaimed gleefully to Brian. "Right on his nose!" The words were still on my lips when there was a boil, a tug and it was on. The fish took off 30 yards of line on its first run, scorching my finger and rather spoiling the stockfish theory. I got him close to the boat and he plunged round, boring deep down when he spotted the waiting net. He towed the boat round in a circle and then round again. Finally he gave up and glided over the net. It was a rainbow of 3lb 6oz, gleaming silver, short and thick and in the sort of condition one expects of Grafham trout. It was to prove the best fish of the day.

By lunchtime we had three fish each, all rainbows, all seen and cast to properly – the cream of the sport. At lunch, with the sun at its height and the lines hanging down limply in the water, we declared a truce. A man with two pounds of sandwiches and two ounces of whisky in him on a drowsy summer's day is as a flower nodding on its stem. Brian's broad back at the other end of the boat, though vertical, had slumber in every line of it and his hat tipped over his eyes suggested that his interest in proceedings had temporarily waned.

A breath of wind caressed our bows, and with a start Brian was galvanised into action. "By Jove. I was almost asleep then." We cruised back to find the ripple where the breeze was filling in from the south.

The weather was changing. On the far horizon, a black cloud grew and grew, eventually looming over the distant house tops like a giant cathedral tower. There was a mutter of thunder. The cloud loomed monstrous and threatening, black as night but surrounded by a watery, pale sky. Surely such a sky will mark the end of the world. The cloud held flickers of lightning, so we changed into oilskins, put our equipment into polythene sacks and waited for the worst. The thunder rose to a continuous crashing. With a roar, the rain fell onto the far end of the lake – we were still dry, but the vertical rods of rain sounded like a waterfall. Great bolts of lightning sizzled downwards and I uneasily recalled that carbon fibre is an ideal conductor.

Then the rain was upon us. One or two great gouts of water at first and then a crashing torrent which flattened the ripple and drummed and bounced on our shoulders. It was a storm of violence such as I have never before witnessed. Doggedly we fished on, for the odd rising fish was still to be seen. I actually took a two-pounder when the storm was at its worst and the boat awash with rain.

Then the storm passed over, leaving a strange, supercharged atmosphere of pale light. The lake steamed and fish rose madly for a quarter of an hour, during which we both caught two more.

It was then that we observed a curious phenomenon. Our flies were just in the surface film, but the nylon between the droppers and the length which led to the flyline was hovering mysteriously above the surface. This apparent defiance of Newton's most famous law was, for a moment, rather disconcerting. Do what we might, the nylon remained levitated, floating in the air like drifting gossamers on a summer morning. This was surely the ideal way to fish surface flies, but the fish had ceased to rise so that we could not capitalise on this unique opportunity of presenting a fly with a completely invisible leader.

After about half-an-hour, the Alice in Wonderland conditions reverted to normal and casts once more fell onto the water in the conventional manner. After long discussion, we concluded that the curious phenomenon had been caused by a sudden change of air temperature after the storm and a strong current of warm air rising from the lake. I wonder if other anglers have ever had this experience? Those who have will vouch for the uncanny and eerie sensation as one of the basic, natural laws is not only broken, but apparently completely reversed.

There were to be two more storms of equal violence and after each one there was a brief and exciting rise of fish. I had three good pulls in as many casts, and on checking the fly I found that the hook had broken at the barb – and that on a fly which had never before today touched water. The time it took to curse and change it was enough for the rise to die away and again I had failed to take proper advantage of the situation. Flies should be checked regularly, especially after one or two fruitless pulls and so, of course, it was all my own fault.

The evening rise did not materialise, for the wind grew mean and cold and the sky lowered angrily round the horizon. We had 14 fish to 3lb 6oz between us and nothing much under 2lb so, with the lights from the village twinkling brightly, we chugged the long way back to the jetty. The same friendly bailiffs were there. "How did you get on? Well done! That's a nice fish." It set the seal on the day.

The one that got away, 6 November 2008

Gracing the river Tweed with his mastery of the double Spey cast, John received a double blow to his hunter-gatherer instincts in this Country Gun column from 2008.

The double Spey cast can be a pretty thing. Line downstream, pick up and roll it on to the surface, high lift, left hand under right pointing upstream, right hand over left downstream and then the firm but controlled roll and punch, aiming high to send the heavy line singing out for the millionth time across the river. Being a slow learner, it took me years to get it right and it feels good when it works, which is not always. Anyone watching has to be impressed, but not the salmon. You could have a Nureyev and David Beckham casting in world champion style and the fish remain unmoved. So there we were, stout boatman and yours truly on Tweed, picking it up and rolling it out, full of hope despite having fished hard on some famous rivers where nary a salmon fell to my wiles and bit of orange tinsel and feather.

Thus it was that from nowhere and without warning 'he' was there, a buzz on the reel, the old war cry from the ancient Hardy Perfect as he screamed away to the far bank and then away downstream. There were savage head shakings, like a bulldog with a wasp, and then a massive leap showering droplets of water that glanced in the weak sun. "Good fish", muttered the gillie, a man not known for overstatement. For ten minutes I battled, and then came signs of weakening. The runs were not quite as long, the tugs lost their savagery and inexorably he was drawn towards the waiting net just as the church clock struck the quarter. He had been on exactly 15 minutes. He saw the netsman standing there and surged away again, a token gesture for now he was done. I drew him slowly inshore when, realising that all was up, he gave a last desperate plunge. There was a ping, the fly fell out, the straining rod flew straight, he wavered a moment in the shallows, righted himself and faded into the peaty water, lost for ever, though how can you lose a thing you never had?

The gillie and I stood in silent dejection, no words would suit the bereavement, though later he permitted himself some observations about my playing of the fish which might, he assured me, have been better, but no recriminations would bring him back. Mournfully we returned to the boat, him rowing to hold us steady in the current, me back in the old routine with the double Spey, pick up, roll, lift, punch, a million and one, a million and two... how many more, I wondered before 'he' was back?

Then the weather stuck its nose in. The beauty of the Spey cast is sullied when you chuck it into a wind strong enough to blow off your deerstalker. Good casters like my sons can do it, but not the out-of-condition writer of these lines. The cast went to pieces, the wheels came off, the fly landed in assorted heaps until in desperation I reverted to the old faithful overhead cast with which I could splash 25 yards on to the pool into the teeth of the gale. That would have to do; the fly whistled past my ear like a rifle bullet as the wind caught it, but at least it was in the water where the salmon were alleged to be. It strengthened, whipping the tops off wavelets, the boat became harder to manage but we stuck to it, working hard, less chatty now, our minds brooding on our tragic loss. How big was it, we wondered? 15, 18 maybe? That lost fish will be a 20-pounder by the weekend; you know how anglers can be.

Lunch was fairly silent, for my companion also was fishless and after it we swapped pools. Halfway down, many casts but fewer than a million later, bless me, there he was again. Buzz, Buzzz...zz, banshee screech of ratchet as off he ran, the 15ft rod arcing, the equal number of stones of Country Gun giving it some muscle. Again a long fight, dogged and powerful and eventually the fish began to wallow, a sign that it was tiring. I would have bet good money that it would follow the other one and escape, for bad luck in fishing comes in batches, but not for the first time I was wrong. The salmon was swallowed in the folds of the great net, lifted gently on to the transom and there she lay to be admired, for it was a hen fish. She had been in the river some time, her silver sea-lustre now faintly coppery after weeks in fresh water. She was full of spawn and ready to lay her eggs. The gillie and I exchanged a glance; no word needed be spoken. I am a hunter-gatherer from way back and love fresh, wild salmon, but her place was back in the river to make lots of babies for anglers who come long after I am gone.

The hook gently removed, she was supported in the water, oxygen sluicing her gills until she shuddered, her great tail wavered and easily she swam out into the stream as good as new. So that was day one. One fish I would have kept but lost, another I released but was safely landed. That, as they say, is fishing.

Steelheads 'n' tales, 5 Sept 2002

With a son based in the US, John eagerly took up the opportunity to cast his line on the Muskegon River, one of many global waters that his career as a writer took him to. In this article from 2002, he discovers the riches of Michigan.

Payback time! After years of shooting and angling at my expense No. 2 son Peter was to host the old man on a fishing expedition, providing the organisation, gillying, transport, licences and tackle. All I had to do was to get my weary, old carcase out to Grand Rapids, Michigan – an easy enough flight from Heathrow, and he would collect me from the airport – and the rest would slip into action like a Swiss watch. This, I had to see.

"It's pretty chilly here, Dad", he had said. "So bring plenty of warm clothes." The cold I enjoy, it is the heat I find hard to handle and, three weeks before, I had been sweating in a Cuban mangrove swamp, shooting blue-winged teal and keeping hostile insects at bay. What was a bit of chill to an old fowler like me? I would relish it.

I got it wrong again for, on day one, it was 10°C below zero, a wind blew straight from the tundra and snow stung the face like a dose of chilled BB. Peter has a house on the Muskegon River and, with typical American generosity, his fishing neighbour, Gerry, sent over a crate of his clobber for me to wear. It must be said that the Yanks have the clothing scene well sussed. I dressed in six layers, each slightly thicker than the one below.

The quarry was steelhead. We all know the good old rainbow trout in our farm ponds, reservoirs and some rivers is as easy to stock as a reared pheasant, quick-growing and sporting enough for most save the pursuit. The steelhead is a truly wild rainbow that lives the life of an Atlantic salmon. They live in the vast sea that is Lake Michigan, within the bounds of which you could lay the whole of Britain. Twice per year, they run up the rivers that seam the state like the veins on a drinker's nose. They come in spring to spawn, and again in autumn to feast on the eggs and fry of the salmon. The steelhead grows to a great size –

fish of more than 30lbs have been recorded – it fights like Rocky Marciano with toothache and is in every respect a truly wonderful fish.

Furthermore, Peter had organised a day with one of the top guides – we call them gillies – on the Muskegon. Respected by his colleagues as a purist and genuine expert, Kevin Feenstra is built like a brick outhouse but, as with many burly men, he is gentle and softly spoken. We were to drop downstream with him in his boat, fishing the pools – they call them holes – with streamer flies with a trout rod and a salmon rod. Kevin is one of three expert guides in the stable of The Great Lakes Fly Fishing Co., a tackle shop in Rockford, Michigan – from which I defy any angler to emerge empty handed – run by the benign Pickwickian figure of Glen Backwood. Glen can lay on the whole package tailored to suit the visitor and, compared to our salmon fishing where success is a long-odds gamble and hotels overpriced, Michigan is astonishingly cheap and you are almost guaranteed fish.

As he readied the boat and loaded the barbecue equipment, Kevin drawled, "I had a day streamer-fishing when the steelhead were fresh out of the lake in the middle of November. The day before, I had eight or nine fish by myself, so I picked up another guide up north and we caught fish on just about every cast it seemed. A couple of spots with big, fresh, chrome fish. Real excitable fish – a great day."

We pushed out on to a wide-bosomed river with wooded banks reminiscent of the lower reaches of the Tay. Snow lay thin on the banks, and a gang of wild turkeys flew raggedly across, like many blown bin liners. Woodpeckers hammered in the larches, and a lone bald eagle beat majestically upstream. Swallows kissed the water dodging snowflakes and three white-tailed deer watched us nervously. I tied on one of Kevin's own flies – a big fluffy thing called an Emulator Sculpin, a sculpin being a small fish. It was a gaudy concoction of wood duck feathers, opossum fur and grizzly marabou.

To sport with your son is a delight that only fathers will know, and the chat and the 'bonding' was as good as the fishing. We dropped downstream easily, Kevin giving us a touch on the oars until we happened on one of his secret pools where he dropped anchor – hands like coat scuttles lowering a mass of chains as though it were thread.

We passed other boats with guides taking out anglers. There was always time to stop for a chat, holding the boat in the stream and talking fishing when a steelhead takes, it is a sudden, solid thud, and then heavy resistance and searing runs. To fight such powerful fish in a strong current was thrilling, and I feared for the tackle. These fish have tails like garden spades and are solid muscle – a world away from the best rainbow you will encounter in the UK. After five minutes of pumping and winding, the monster rolls a bar of silver or, as they say over there, 'chrome', and with a deft swoop of the giant net, it is thrashing in the boat. Catch-and-release is standard practice, a small one might go home for the pan, but the things you can do with six 10lb steelies is limited.

The line kept freezing in the rod rings. Suddenly, the casting snarled up and there was an ice nugget in each of the top five. I had read in a Victorian salmon-fishing book that when the rings froze, you instructed your gillie to thaw them in his mouth. I felt that Kevin might not be receptive to such a proposal, so I cracked the icicles with my thumbnail.

It is stupendous sport and the fishing is free, once you have your licence – less than a fiver per day for non-residents. Unlike over here, the original settlers decided that the rivers and mountains should not be privately owned and the sport on them was for the people. I might suggest the idea to the owner of the Junction Pool on Tweed. The only cost is the guide, the accommodation and the flight, which, in these days of the internet, is a competitive business. To fish for a week on a moderate Scottish river plus accommodation could set you back £2,000. On the Michigan rivers, assuming two anglers, you can get by with about £100 per rod per day for the guide. In the USA, a dollar will buy what a pound will buy, eateries are plentiful, good and cheap and the people delightfully welcoming and hospitable. They want you to have a good time. You may fish any method, for the fly is not compulsory, but the guide will advise on the style for the day.

With easy strokes on the oars, Kevin pulled to the shore for lunch – a sweeping bend of pebbly beach with a towering, tree-clad bluff on the far side of the river. Red-tailed hawks wheeled and mewed. Kevin got the barbecue going with a roar and soon had a row of sausages sizzling nicely. Washed down by a few Buds, it was a timely and pleasant pause for reflection in a stunningly beautiful place.

It was good to fish with a real expert, but for the rest of the week,

Peter and I were on our own, joined sometimes by his friend Tom Darling, both of them experienced and skilled river anglers. We caught several more steelhead, up to 15lbs, and on the last day, we tried the Grand River that runs through the suburbs of Grand Rapids. We eased the boat into the maelstrom below the weir where the fish stack up, unable to ascend further. There were other anglers out, three other boats and a score or so fishing from the shore, perched on rocks like so many cormorants. This was our best day, for swinging downstream from an anchored boat, we took 17 fish between us. Some were coloured, having been in the river a while, but the majority were gleaming 'chrome' – you see, I was getting used to the terminology. All our fish were returned, and from watching other anglers, that seemed to be the custom.

Michigan is a fishing heaven, for the rivers have sport on offer in most months of the year. As well as two steelhead runs, there is brown trout fishing to die for, great fish rising to the dry fly and, during the hatch of the hex, a giant mayfly, it is probably some of the best in the world. The river also has runs of king salmon, so there is something special to catch in every month of the year. In my view, steelhead fishing in Michigan throws down the gauntlet to much Scottish salmon fishing.

Amazonian adventures, 4 January 2001

Piranhas, anacondas and monkeys – John's trip to Bolivia in 2000, recounted in this Country Gun column, saw him an awfully long way from home.

"Whatever you do," said Wyatt, "don't cast your fly anywhere near one of those chaps." With a wave of his arm he indicated a knobbly log with bulging eyes lying stone still in the water hyacinth. It was a cayman, and he seemed to have the potential for a bad attitude. I kept my flies well away from those leathery backs and bottle-green, impassive eyes.

To this day I am not too sure exactly where we were, save that it was certainly in Bolivia in the upper waters of the Rio Grande and Amazon where tributaries wind like a nest of corn snakes. Gripping with one hand the side of the dugout canoe, I trained the glasses on this bird or that, but magnifying power was unnecessary – they were close enough to touch with a long pole. Every ivy-clad stump had its own eagle, hawk, harrier or falcon.

Kingfishers of different sizes and gaudy liveries flew ahead with shrill whistles. Macaws in their finery of red, yellow, blue and green sailed shrieking across from this dead tree to that, fanned their impossible tails and chuckled at us as we passed below. In beds of water hyacinth, flamingo-pink spoonbills waded delicately, storks stood on stilt legs and small bitterns crept like gnomes beneath the riverside bushes. Gosh, its good here.

Having shot the eared doves once or twice earlier, it was time to lay aside the gun and take up the rod. There is a limit to how many days of dove shooting a chap can stand, though the doves were so numerous that they were undisturbed by our depredations.

Now the rod was to become mightier than the gun and we were after peacock bass, a muscly, stripy bruiser; a cross between a bass and a perch with sandpaper teeth and a chip on his shoulder. Hurl out a coarse, pop-eyed fly tied for me by Farlows, splash it down, let it sink a few inches and strip back. The peacock bass does not care for anything, no matter how small, trespassing in its territory. From the thickest of the water hyacinth there comes a swirl, then a bow wave rips in like an attacking shark. Hypnotised by the sight, you slow down the stripping arm. "Keep going, keep going!" shouts Wyatt. With an explosion on the surface and a savage pull you find you have him on. A series of searing runs follows and at last he is hauled into the stern, his mouth, into which you could insert a cricket ball, gulping angrily. The Indian guide dons a teflon glove and seizes a pair of rat-tailed pliers. He grabs the fish, holds it aloft, removes the hook and slips it back into the water. The hooks are barbless, and catch and release is the policy. Being so aggressive, the fish are not hard to catch and to take 100 in a day was not unknown. They can run to 20lb in weight.

Once we were out on a huge lake, Guachuna, in which you could lose an English county. No gringo had fished there before. Two miles from shore, I realised that the guide was baling with his baseball cap, a storm was on the way, the lake was heaving with piranhas and goodness knows what else and we had no mobile phone between us, but the fishing was well worth the adventure, for it was superb.

Back at camp we ate and drank well and watched out for the giant anaconda which a week before had eaten one of the camp dogs. Nightly strolls became the more interesting for his presence. The camp also boasted a clutch of orphaned macaws and a tamed spider monkey named Maria. I got on famously with her and would happily have taken her home. Maybe she recognised a kindred spirit or even, as someone remarked unkindly, a relation.

It was a wonderful adventure and so eventful that it would take a small book of its own to tell it all. There is no time to tell of the freshwater dolphins that reared and plunged as we surged up the brown rivers. It would take a page to describe how the passengers pushed a twin-engine plane out of the mud before we could take off, and of the landing strip which they made by driving a bulldozer through 30 miles of equatorial jungle.

The heat was akin to a boiled blanket being dropped firmly onto the bonce and yet none of us ailed or faded. I would like to have told you off the rheas which ran long-legged and stately through fields of sunflowers. I could describe the small plane being beaten back by a hurricane and running out of fuel, making an unscheduled stop in a tiny town on carnival night and us joining in the fun. The kindness of everyone we met, often people who had few material possessions, was a lesson not to be forgotten.

There's no harm in glancing back over the shoulder to hot days, especially now when we plug on in the depths of a wet British winter. If we seize the opportunities, our fieldsports have many rich adventures to offer.

Victory in the second test, 15 April 2004

Swapping delicate chalkstream fishing in Hampshire for bigger stuff off the back of a boat in Barbados, John quickly worked out that deep-sea fishing was a somewhat scarier proposition.

Deep-sea big-game fishing has as much in common with my day-to-day trouting as sumo wrestling does with needlepoint. Forget your little Hardy 5-weight wand, horsehair leader and fly like a scrap of navel fluff. In the sea off Barbados you need a rod the length and thickness of a broom handle, 200lb leader and a reel that looks as if it had been designed by Harland and Woolf. You play your fish not with wrist pressure but strapped into a chair bolted to the deck with the butt of the rod jammed into a cup fixed between your knees. Both quarry are of the genus pisces but there the resemblance ends.

At the needlepoint end you test yourself with a dainty spotted trout weighing a pound or so. For the sumo brigade it is a fish as big and strong as you, often more so. Blue marlin, sailfish, wahoo or kingfish, yellowfin tuna and barracuda are in the tag wrestling team. There are tales of a 1,000lb fish being played for a day. My companion that day told me of the wire man, the chap with a stout glove who pulls the wire leading to the mouth of a beaten fish so that it may be released or gaffed. Being new to the job he wrapped the trace round his hand –

fatal. The marlin flapped, the main line broke and the great fish dragged the chap with the wire locked round his knuckles into the water and towed him into the depths. Neither was seen again. You get none of that on the Test.

The Caribbean glittered wine dark ahead, aquamarine astern. Waves pitched and tossed, flying fish like swallows skimmed the troughs hunted by a brown booby which dodged wake like the albatross in The Ancient Mariner. Perched high in his eyrie the captain drove the boat at a steady five knots, and on the deck Henderson the mate saw to the needs of the two fishermen. Henderson was quick as lightning about The Blue Jay. He had two rods on outriggers and two others fishing deep. He nipped about checking reel drag, adjusting an outrigger or changing a bait.

Once my companion's rod gave a bounce and Henderson was across the boat and had snatched it before the fisherman a yard away had stretched out a hand. The bait came in sliced as if by a razor. Henderson and I got off on the wrong foot. I put my hand on the line just above the reel, letting it lie over my palm to feel the tension. Henderson scolded me. A fish might take at any point, and if it happened while my hand was there the line would amputate my fingers in a flash. "If you do it again while I am not looking, at least you were warned," he said.

Duly rebuked, I lounged in the chair sniffing diesel fumes, rolling with the boat, sipping a Banks Barbadian beer and watching the white sand a mile away. An hour passed – my rod jagged sharply, Henderson's hand and mine hit the butt but I gave way to the guv'nor. He struck mightily, once, twice and thrice, the muscles on his back standing out like knotted rope. He jammed the butt into the cup.

"Wind in," he commanded.

"I can't," I said, trying.

"If I say wind in, then wind it."

I did, but the line came slowly, often running out and losing hard-won yards. The trick is to keep on the pressure – these fish are good at shedding the hook. The pumping left hand fighting the boat as well as the fish grew numb so I rested and changed arms, holding the fish steady How anyone can play one of these brutes for an hour let alone a day beats me.

After an age, the rubber band on the line showing I had only 30yds out came slowly down the rings. Henderson got ready a gaff big enough to heft one-ton straw bales. The beaten fish was under the stern, though from my seat I could not see it. Henderson snapped at me to slacken off a bit, bent over, there was a cobra strike, a heave and into the boat he drew this apparition like a giant mackerel with teeth, a wahoo or kingfish, five feet long. It glowed with inner fires, lavender, pink and apple green, delicate bars of brown on its flanks. The moment it hit the sun-drenched deck its flame went out. Deftly Henderson removed the hook but he was still on my case.

"Keep away from those teeth", he said. "They are like a razor. The bite of a dead one is worse than a live one."

That fish would do me, but then I caught a barracuda. Henderson mellowed and when I pressed into his palm a piece of green paper bearing the head of George Washington we were pals. Back at the hotel I was briefly a hero and my fish featured a la carte for two nights, though I was disappointed not to merit a byline. Exciting and good fun but more hard labour than sport. I think I will stick to the spotted trout; less danger of a rupture and of being pulled in.

Country Gun, 26 October 2011

For most participants, fieldsports are a shared passion with enthusiasm handed down from generation to generation. In one of John's final Country Gun columns, he recounted a truly momentous family occasion.

I promised eager readers to tell all about our famous salmon fishing day, so brace yourselves. I had written up my season in this column fairly accurately, but there are only so many ways of saying 'we caught nothing'. Nevertheless, we were grateful to seize a few crumbs along the way in the form of pulls, lost fish, foul hooks and kelts.

It is a long road that has no turning, and the thing about salmon fishing is keeping the fly in the water – for that is the one that catches most fish. Also, hold the thought that every cast you make is one closer to your next fish. It all came together prophetically. Hearing about my little medical indisposition, No. 2 son Peter flew in from Michigan, just happening to bring a little rod with him. No. 1 son David was delayed in his potato harvest by wet ground, and No. 1 grandson, Max William, was on his school holidays. It was the end of August, so all the Humphreys men assembled on the banks of the majestic Tweed – which was full with salmon – all there to sport at my expense. Also, there was the second rod, my friend John, but he was alone – only the Humphreys were mob-handed.

Day one of three was a bit odd, for the water was high but falling. The salmon were running, and a running fish does not take like a resting one, which hooks far better. John landed a nice 10-pounder, and I had four on, one after the other, but they all came unstuck – partly the story of my season and partly because they were badly hooked. The next day the water was ideal, and shortly after starting I landed a fine 16-pound cock fish – nice and clean and perfect for sending to the smokery. An old hunter-gatherer does not turn down such chances, and as I have killed no fish in living memory, this was the opportunity to stock up.

I got another shortly after and then the two sons fished, both landing salmon, so all were happy. Grandson Max had fished half a dozen times with his little rod with a spinner, but so far he had never had a touch. Usually salmon are not easy, and his attention span is limited, running on a good day to about half an hour. He had been christened in Tweed water, so the dear old river might have had a soft spot for him. The kindly head boatman, Brendan, invited him to have a couple of chucks and he did not need asking twice. His father was in the boat with him and the rest of the admiring family clustered on the bank.

Then the impossible happened – the little rod was bent into a C and a lovely salmon dashed off. Max not being up to the dark arts of pumping and winding, the fight was a bit one-sided – the salmon having the best of it. It towed the boat and the three humans inside downstream, while Max put his foot on the transom to brace himself to maintain the pressure. Even the biggest salmon in the world cannot take much of that, but it was a quarter of a mile downstream before Brendan came ashore and readied the net.

Even then there were anxious moments as the fish made a few wild dashes for freedom, but the net was expertly slid underneath him and a clean 7½lb salmon was lifted triumphantly aloft. The crowd on the bank cheered so wildly that John – out of sight round the corner in the other boat – said later it sounded like the winning goal in a Cup Final. Max groped in his bag for his new staghorn priest, which he wielded with gusto and then christened.

Two happy things about the adventure were that, firstly, the fish was fairly small – a lad catching a monster for his first one is wrong, for how can he follow it with a better? Secondly, it was far from his first attempt, having tried many times before without success, so he had learned that salmon do not come easily and that this one was to be appreciated.

That night the fish was cooked at his house and, as founder of the feast, he sat at the head of the table, accepting the plaudits of the diners. Another little piece of serendipity was that he had asked a week before for a book to enter his shooting and fishing expeditions in – still rare events but due to become more frequent, and the earliest entries are often the most fun. Accordingly, I presented him with my Country Sportsman's Record Book and Journal the day before, so the momentous first salmon was his first entry. If you had set out to write the perfect fishing story from your imagination, you could not have done it better.

Thus it was that all the Humphreys men landed salmon on the same day, sharing one rod. All witnessed Max's first fish, and what could be better than that? One thing was for sure, as a tonic to a sick man, it beat all the bottles of medicine ever concocted, and I still lie awake at night thinking about it.

The Fens

Throughout his life, John identified himself
as a product of the fens. To many they
are the flatlands of the east, but to
him they were a landscape that held
a fascinating history and were host
to a cast of rebels and not a few rogues.
In the fens, he certainly felt at home.

Fen showy, Country Life, *27 April 2007*

Are the fens bleak and forbidding or one of the country's greatest treasures? It's a bit of both. In one of his earliest Countryman columns for Country Life, *John explained why they are so special.*

'The wide, wide fens are drear and cold
And drear and cold the weather
But the skies are light and the fens are bright
When warm hearts meet together.'

I t is tempting to just accelerate through it. The straight roads innocent of commuter traffic encourage speed and the motorist 'from furrin parts' is seduced into stepping on the gas and turning up the radio until he has left the flat fen far behind. That driver misses much. The delights of what the Victorian diarist Dugdale called 'this hideous fen of huge bigness' are subtle and acquired. Anyone may stand at the foot of an Alp and gawp, but the fen is mysterious, sinister and desolate. From the slumbering lust of the crawling tideways to the lonely reed beds where the wind blows, will-o'-the-wisps dance and strange birds wail, it touches deep places in the soul. Here are shining dykes laid across the land like sword blades, shock-haired willows march along the droves like dwarfish sentinels. The soil is black as a yard up a chimney and grows record crops; lean on a walking stick and it sprouts leaves. Much of the fen is below sea level and here and there are the remains of a drainage mill, one of 700 that clacked round, scooping the water from one level to another.

You happen on lonely hamlets innocent of architectural aspiration, home to a creeping breed of mongrel Britons, 'Fen Tigers' they called them, not for their ferocity, but as a corruption of 'Fen Dykers'. They were said to have yellow-spotted bellies, webbed feet and passed their lives high on poppy-head tea, laudanum laced with brandy to keep off the ague. They scythed the tawny-tasselled Norfolk reeds for thatching, poled their flat-bottomed punts, and with long brown guns hunted the teeming wildfowl that rose from distant meres with the sound of thunder. They harvested eels with flat-bladed glaives, hives, grigs and fyke nets and speared pike and bream with tools the Saxons brought with them. They herded scrawny cattle on the river washes, dug peat and skated in winter, the little village of Welney alone producing a run of world champions. They washed when they fell into a dyke, wore muslin bags on their heads to keep off mosquitoes, and brawled in the pubs. One of the favourite recreations was shin kicking on Fore Hill in Ely on a Saturday. An old-timer recalled: "I rec'llect the losers being carried away on turf barrows". He wiped away a tear. "Thim was gay old toimes…"

They built some of the most magnificent abbeys and churches in the fair land of England, long fingers reaching up to heaven on a flat land of no natural stone. Many were built in the 14th century of gritty Barnack rag, each block ferried by water from the quarry near Peterborough, hauled up the greensand slope by horsepower and swung aloft with block and tackle. In times of trouble, the bells clanged out their timeless warning: 'Fire, Flood, Foes, Awake, Awake.' It might have been Vikings in raven-beaked warships stealing up the winding rivers or melt water rushing down from the Midlands to flood their hovels. To this day, there is rivalry between two fen villages, one claiming, 'Thim lot never told us the Danes were coming.' You don't forget a thing like that.

The great lantern of Ely cathedral is the most striking fenland house of God, its pointing arm a benediction and a landmark for travellers in the old Isle of Ely before the Dutchmen drained it. The name Ely derives from helig, the Saxon word for a willow and nothing to do with eels. Thereabouts, Hereward fought a guerrilla campaign against William's mail-clad Normans, firing the reeds so their tawny flames and acrid smoke engulfed the invaders. The only reason the cathedral city fell after a long siege was through treachery, and Hereward escaped by boat.

Bitterns were so common that they were a favourite Sunday dinner in many a turf hut. Hawks, harriers and otters swarmed and clamouring skeins of countless wildfowl peppered the heavens like copper coins shot from a gun. Today, the tiny fen pheasants are the most sporting in the land, brought over by 'thim owd Roomans', whose ghosts still haunt the lonely places. The vast bosom of Whittlesey Mere near Peterborough was a playground for the rich who came for regattas and pike fishing. They collected fen butterflies, including the swallowtail and the now-extinct large copper. The largest eel and the greatest pike in England came from that water. 'Such were the giants of Huntingdonshire in olden times' reads the legend above a carving of the monstrous fish.

Those living round the lake in wet times built fires on bricks in the hearth and their horses ploughed with boards strapped to their hooves. They drained it with a new machine called Appold's Pump, a centrifugal device shown first at the Great Exhibition of 1850. In a week, it achieved what generations of Dutchmen in their iron-shod clogs and English money had managed to only partly achieve. The locals had never cared for the Dutchmen under Cornelius Vermuyden who had drained away the water, and with it, the fish and ducks on which they depended. They murdered them, threw their bodies in their own dykes and blew up the new sluices with gunpowder.

That land became the richest farmland in England, but its fortunes fluctuated. In the depression of the 1930s, small farmers paid more to grow a crop than they got for it at market. Broken-hearted, they emigrated in droves and halfway across the Atlantic threw their deeds into the ocean. Those who followed after the war simply adopted the abandoned holdings.

Whole village populations were once were supported by one large farm, a typical 1,000-acre holding employing 40 men. As technology improved and wages rose, the same acreage could be worked by two men with great machines. Finally, even they went, and contractors came in from afar and blitzed the land using 10-furrow ploughs and enormous seed drills, before vanishing from the community until spraying time, leaving the wild acres lonely and silent.

Today, many fields lie fallow as although carrots in the supermarket cost much the same as ever, grow a field of them in the fen and you're lucky if they go for horse food; many are ploughed in. The old staples of cereals and sugar beet hang on by a thread, although recent price rises in wheat hold out a glimmer of hope to beleaguered farmers. The development of biofuel from straw and willow needs Government initiatives to really take off. Ethanol fuel from farm crops is another possible lifeline, following news that, in the USA, they are devoting a high percentage of their maize land to that end. Herbs, mushrooms, beetroot, daffodils, asparagus, fishing lakes and livery stables all hold hope. A nagging worry is that the once-bottomless peat and silt have shrunk due to oxidisation, wind and drainage. In some places, it is mere inches away from the unproductive clay beneath.

The National Trust intends to buy a great tract of land in the Cambridgeshire Wicken Fen area and revert it to the watery wilderness of Hereward that we spent 300 years draining. If that occurs, there will be ironic chuckles from the watery graves of many an old Fen Tiger, but at least the farming problem will have been solved.

The peat and silt are laced with bog oak, ossified trees that last grew leaves when the aurochs, beaver and wolf roamed. The great skies are timeless, the vast, domed vault of the heavens accentuated by the low horizons, so flat that you can see the curvature of the earth. See those bloodshot skies reflected in jumbled floodwater, shiver in a wind zipping uninterrupted from the Urals, watch distant skeins of fowl toiling into a gale and you'll soon sense that you're an intruder in a waterland wrested from nature, liable to be surrendered to her at any moment.

Is this a land through which to drive willy-nilly without a second thought, car radio and heater at full blast, striving to depart from it as quickly as possible? Surely not.

Fenland decoys, 16 July 1985

When we think of decoys, shooters tend to think of plastic dummies or dead pigeons, but in this historical piece from **Shooting Times** *in 1985, John explored the historical operation of the fenland duck decoys which were capable of harvesting thousands of ducks in one go.*

I consider it a rare stroke of luck to have known two decoymen in my life. One is Don Revitt who, for years, ran the decoy at Nacton in Suffolk and the other, Tony Cook, who is still in charge of the one at Borough Fen in Cambridgeshire. Both decoys are used now as demonstration pieces, relics of an age that has passed, final remnants of what was once a flourishing industry throughout the country, but especially in East Anglia. The duck caught by this ancient method are today ringed and released for research purposes, a rather more pleasant fate than that suffered by their ancestors when the decoys were, as originally intended, worked to supply the London poultry markets.

Driving duck into nets placed there to catch them was a very ancient practice, done in late summer or early autumn when parent mallard and their well-grown ducklings were flightless in eclipse plumage. Nets were set along many hundreds of yards of shoreline and every able-bodied man, woman, child and dog was called upon for the drive; every leaky and crazy boat, punt, raft or indeed anything that would float and carry a passenger well enough for one traverse of the lake was pressed into service. The birds were flushed from the reedbeds by dogs and men armed with sticks, and driven onto the open water. On some of the great undrained Fen meres such as Whittlesea, the flock might have amounted to several thousand fowl which drew together in a great raft, acres in extent, out on the winking ripples.

In 1432, a wild gang of half-starved, desperate Fen tigers ran a net along the pond of the Abbot of Crowland and took 600 birds in one go. This was a small, local, impromptu effort when set against the 3,000 mallard taken in a single, well-orchestrated and carefully planned drive on a lake up Spalding way, or the 4,000 taken in 1720 at Deeping Fen or the 3,000 taken in the same place two days later. It was a great slaughter but duck drives of this sort were seasonal, opportunist affairs, heavy on manpower and liable to go wrong. The proper decoy was a refinement, a subtly devised, terrible machine for duck destruction on a scale never attained before or since.

Its deadly simplicity relied on the natural law which dictates that wildfowl will mob, or at least swim close, to investigate a fox on the bank. This habit was their undoing, and because of it, ducks by the 10,000 could be taken from a pond by one man without the firing of a shot or even the duck left on the water being aware that anything was amiss. The method of operation is too well-known to require a further thesis from me, but for anyone who may just have returned from a life spent in Kurdistan (those not in that category may skip the rest of the paragraph), may I explain briefly that the duck, attracted by a glimpse of the 'coyman's foxy dog, swam towards it, the dog appearing each time a little further off up a large, netted tunnel which narrowed and imperceptibly curved away from the main pond. Hidden behind a series of reed screens, the decoyer worked his dog, usually named Piper, and when the 'fowl had been drawn well down the pipe, he ran back, flushed them and drove them into a net at the end of the tunnel. He removed the birds, wrung their necks and took them to the larder. Each pond had not one, but a series of pipes, so that the decoyman could use the wind to his advantage and work the pipe with the biggest concentration of birds near it.

The dead 'fowl were hung in a cool, airy, stone building in a shady part of the wood. Go now to Nacton and force your way through the nettles, heave open the door and allow your eyes to grow accustomed to the gloom and, on the hottest, stillest summer day, the cool air will feel like a balm on your forehead. Then you see row upon row of rusty hooks, rank above rank, level upon level on every wall, uncountable, unless you have an hour to spare. Perforated bricks, shrewdly placed, ensure a flow of fresh air; at floor level, drainpipes driven through the walls show where cold water could be run over the flagged floor to further lower the temperature in an especially hot spell. Things had to be thus in 1830, as the electric cold store and the deep-freeze were matters for the undreamed-of future.

The birds were taken there, piled high on a flat barrow, packed thence onto a horse and cart, taken to the station and rushed down to London and the Leadenhall Street Market. In hot weather, many of the birds must have been rather high by the time they reached the table. Horses were foaled, broken, worked, grew grey and died of old age doing no more than ferrying wildfowl from the decoy to the London train.

The sheer size of the bags taken by this means is difficult for us today to conceive, for the Fens were partly flooded and heaving with wildfowl. The decoy ponds were carefully situated to take advantage of flightlines and natural concentrations of the birds; they were planted round with trees to provide shelter and seclusion, strict privacy was enforced and it was a punishable offence to fire a gun within one mile downwind and two miles upwind of a decoy, a law probably still on the statute books. Unsuspecting duck would find the pond a haven of peace and plenty with corn scattered in the shallows, no sign of a human being, no noise, protection from the nor'easterlies and plenty of companionship of their own kind.

It is little wonder that Fen farmers and land-owners found that a judiciously-placed pond on their holding was vastly more profitable than a few acres of scrubby barley or a flock of scraggy sheep. A pond was easily dug and a good man quickly found to work the pipes and start the income flowing. Tom Williams, the Lakenheath decoyman, cleared £700 in a single year, a princely revenue when the Old Queen had just succeeded. When Sir Ralph Payne Gallwey researched and mapped decoys and wrote, in 1886, his famous *Book of Duck Decoys*, he recorded a rash of them in the Fens and along the east coast – the not atypical village of Wainfleet in Lincolnshire, for example, had no less than five active decoys, so their combined national financial turnover must have been considerable.

The same Tom Williams sent from Lakenheath a ton of ducks twice a week when the decoy was working flat out. 'Fowl sat out on the surrounding Fen, waiting to pile into the pond. A keeper in 1878 recorded fully 3,000 wildfowl sitting out on the marshes, waiting for those inside to be taken to make room for them. The decoy was so full that it looked as if one could not prick a pin in between them. That decoy once took 15,000 duck in one season.

The Ashby decoy took, over 35 consecutive seasons, nearly 100,000 'fowl, comprising 48,664 mallard, 44,568 teal, 2,019 wigeon, 285 shoveler, 278 pintail and 22 gadwall. The best single year was 1834-35 when 6,357 birds were taken. Consider that these figures refer to only one of many hundreds of working decoys and it paints a picture not only of the monumental slaughter, but of the well-nigh incalculable stocks of wildfowl in the Fens at the time.

Two tons of wildfowl went to market each week; 15,000 duck in a season from one decoy, 6,000 from another, 4,000 from a third and a 35-year 'take' of 100,000 birds from a fourth – such was the simple arithmetic of the commercial decoys which once speckled the map of East Anglia. The ill-drained marshy fens were so full of 'fowl that one chronicler recalled duck almost queueing up to take shelter on the decoy pond, but held up simply because the 'coyman could not take them fast enough and there was not room on the water for another bird. During that week the 'coyman made take after take, running his 'piper' dog until it was weary, culling, driving, untying the net, breaking nets and pushing the groaning barrow to the larder until he too was exhausted.

The old-time decoyman was a respected citizen in the village, a person of standing and prosperity who could afford to have his portrait painted in oils and hung in his own hall. After all, he was a steady source of revenue for his employer and his skills and productivity were properly rewarded. Don Revitt was 'coyman at Nacton, a slight departure from the tradition which saw the job passed from father to son over many generations. In Don's case, the decoying line lay on his wife's side of the family and his father-in-law, old Tom, who, at the age of 90, could swing a scythe and hang on to a swaying ladder while repairing the netting in a pipe, and put to shame many a younger man. He could, if he wished, tell a tale or two, but he wouldn't, for the customary close keeping of the secrets of the decoyer's art dies hard. Nacton was a famous decoy, noted for its pintail and teal, but the formation of new reservoirs and changes in the local geography of the coastline caused the 'fowl to dwindle and change their habits. During its last few years the decoy had been operated by the Wildfowl Trust and the 'fowl ringed and released, but now it is run by the Suffolk Naturalists Trust, and Don and his family, not forgetting Piper the dog, moved down to the Wildfowl Trust refuge at Welney where Don took a job as the Warden.

Tony Cook works the Borough Fen decoy as a demonstration piece and he has inherited the traditions of one of the most famous names in the history of decoying. It was the Williams family which ran the decoy for many generations, Annie Williams, sister of the late 'coyman Billy Williams, is still sprightly, also a nonagenarian but, unlike Tom, she is full of tales of the old days, for she herself was much happier 'playing the pipes' than playing with dolls. Decoy folk generally seem to have been long lived, for old Tom Williams was 109 when he died and they said he would have been good for another decade had he not suffered the misfortune of falling into a frozen dyke when he had a sack of duck on his back. At its peak, the Borough Fen decoy was taking a regular 15,000 duck in a season.

Borough Fen was surrounded by many natural meres and winding Fen waterways, not least the huge mere at Whittlesea over which the wildfowl and above them the hawks, ospreys. harriers and kites were said to have blackened the sky. There was an apparently endless reserve of birds from which the decoys could draw. It was in 1670 that permission was sought by Mr Williams, acting as agent to the Earl of Lincoln, to draw water from the Riser Welland to top up the decoy pond; early attempts at drainage may have been responsible for a lowering of the water table. Even at that early date the decoy was already a going concern and the Williams family were established as 'coymen, and that 300 years ago. The family prospered and sent out its cadets to run decoys elsewhere, Andrew Williams (1692–1776) was an example of one who learned his trade at home and then went to become, for 60 years, 'coyman at Aston Hall in Shropshire, where he died and was given this famous, wry epitaph:

> *'Here lies the decoyman who lived like an otter,*
> *Dividing his time 'twin the land and the water;*
> *His hide he oft soaked in the waters of Perry*
> *While Aston old beer his spirits kept merry.*
> *Amphibious in life. Death was puzzled to say*
> *How to dust reduce such a well moistened clay;*

So Death turned decoyman, and 'coyed him to land,
Where he fixed his abode till quite dry to the hand,
He then found him fitting for crumbling to dust,
And here he lies mouldering as you and I must.'

The Perry was the river which fed the decoy. The decline of the decoys was almost as rapid and spectacular as the fall of the coprolite mining industry. The Fens were drained, a long and spasmodic process, but the result was dry land where there had been marsh and, it was the old story: while the birds could stand the depredations of the decoys, they dwindled to a fraction of their former numbers when the habitat was removed. No longer were there the seemingly endless stocks to fill the decoy ponds and be culled in numbers which, although huge, were a small proportion of uncountable flocks. Where Richard Skelton once took 30 dozen birds (the 'coymen counted their bags in dozens) a day for three days, over a thousand in the week, they built a railway to run past his pond. The birds, already much reduced due to local land reclamation, could not stand the disturbance and they left; the decoy was abandoned.

Decoys had had their day; a changing landscape, a new morality and easy availability of fresh meat caused their swift and predictable decline. An aerial photograph of the Fens will show the shallow depressions in the wheatfields where the ponds once lay. A careful searcher may still find, in a baking, midsummer fen, an unexpected oasis, a forgotten, quiet pond surrounded by old, leaning willows and choked with rush. If he is especially lucky, he may discover in the nettles the rusty metal stubs which show where stood the footings of the great arches of the pipe mouths.

That is all that remains, together with a few old chronicles, bag records and account books, and also the memories of the likes of Annie Williams and old Tom who will keep safely his secrets. The old 'coyman's duck barrow is displayed in the local folk museum as a curiosity. However, Tony Cook and Don Revitt are still young men; possibly no one of their generation knows as much of the practical side of decoys and decoying together with the tricks of that curious trade than they. Their arts depended on using one simple deception; they called for no punt gun, array of beaters nor battery of mechanical devices to take stupendous bags of duck but, as I once heard an old Fenman say, they 'took their buds natural'. They were great fieldcraftsmen with an encyclopaedic knowledge of the ways of wildfowl. To end this short account where I began it, I count myself proud to know them both, for in their company I somehow feel closer to a chapter of wildfowling history which has now passed.

Carrots and potatoes grow where the will-o'-the-wisp once capered yellowly over the steaming morasses; the phut-putting of tractors and the drone of combine-harvesters fill the flat silences where once the wildfowl rose with a roar like distant thunder.

High in the Fens, 18 February 1988

Mention the drug trade, and the names that spring to mind are Miami and Bogota not Wisbech and St Ives, but as John showed in this article from 1988, East Anglia had its fair share of Fen tigers in search of a fix.

Just back from the marsh on one of those dead evenings of mist and brooding silence. Sitting alone in the rushes I could swear I sensed Nature breathing and could feel her slow, steady pulse. In fact it was far from silent for, as the evening advanced and even the pearl grey light leaked from the sky, the little sounds were all about me, magnified and distorted by a billion tiny droplets.

The thin squeal of the water rail made me start, the rapid wing beats of a pochard flying upriver sounded like the rasp of sandpaper, violently and rhythmically applied. A brief burst of Canada music broke out far off and was, as suddenly, stilled. Invisible wigeon, mallard and teal all called; little rustlings were close enough to be disconcerting. With a startling eruption and choleric chortling, a cock pheasant flew up to roost in the thorn. He had larynx trouble, for he rounded off each full-blooded burst of cackling with a most unpleasant-like croak, rather like a chicken.

Other pheasants far and near went up fussily... how could I have searched so hard an hour ago and stumbled on only one? Even that was a strong runner which scuttled over the floodbank so quickly as to bewilder the eye, but Kenzie was hot on its tail and I heard his triumphant crash in the bushes on the far side. Those birds now blundering so conspicuously up into the trees had learned the art of self-effacement when it mattered.

In near darkness I splashed off the marsh, skirting the deeps, forcing a path through wet and clinging Norfolk reed and blessing my stars that I knew the way. I had two mallard, a pheasant and a moorhen in the bag at the cost of two cartridges; Kenzie had caught the moorhen and pegged one of my tame mallard – he likes to do his bit. It was then that I began to appreciate the need of 18th century Fen folk to consume opium to an extent that was so high as to attract national consternation.

A wet, dank, ill-drained, marshy world lay at the root of it: medical assistance was limited, especially for the poor and the majority of the population was prone to argue, 'painful rheumatisms and neuralgia'. The result was, according to a public health report of the time that, '... there was not a labourer's house... without its penny stick or pill of opium and not a child that did not have it in some form'. More opium was sold in Cambridgeshire and Lincolnshire than in any other part of the country.

Poppyhead tea was a regular elixir in the Fens. The Burwell historian, the late Dr Lucas, reported that, 'a patch of white poppies was usually found in most of the Fen gardens. Poppyhead tea was in frequent use, and was taken as a remedy for ague and was given to children during the teething period.' My own Fen vegetable patch, sited on the gardens of demolished 18th-century cottages, still boasts a patch of these poppies which have survived a century of agricultural operations. There was once even an attempt made in Norfolk to produce opium on a commercial scale.

The death rate from opium poisoning in the Fens was higher than in the most run-down inner city. In 1863, Sir John Simon, Medical Officer to the Privy Council, wrote of a Fenman who complained that his wife had spent £100 on opium since they married, of a labourer seen asleep leaning on his hoe and of the standard practice of never drinking beer unless a piece of opium had been dropped into it first. The drug offered relief from the scourges of poverty, rheumatism and ague. The Isle of Ely, Whittlesey, Kings Lynn, St Ives, Methwold, Burwell, Soham and Holbeach were centres of the addiction. A friend of a patient whose symptoms had baffled the new doctor soon put him right: "Lor, Sir! She has had a shillingsworth of laudanum since yesterday morning."

A Wisbech druggist reported, '...daily I supply a vast number with either opium or laudanum ... the amount consumed is enormous'. On a Saturday evening the chemists' shops were crowded with folk who would lay down their money and receive the pills in exchange without a word being spoken. The 'opium slaves' of Croyland (near Peterborough) would buy a shillingsworth made up of 20 good-sized pills and consume them in one go on the spot.

Charles Kingsley in *Alton Locke* described the 'ven-man's wife' calling for her 'pennard of elevation to last her out the week. It keeps the women-folk quiet, so it do...' The drug was also used on pigs which 'fatted better when kept from crying', on sheep and horses, but especially to keep babies quiet. Infant mortality at Wisbech ran at 206 per 1,000; one woman took 96 grains a day, others would take the dose before the very eyes of the startled chemist. A single chemist sold 200lb of opium in a year while in 1859 the Fenland total consumption was estimated at over 3,000,000lb. In time, not only chemists but every high street shop had its counter piled high with vials of what was known as 'the stuff'. At a cost of up to sixpence an ounce in Ely, the money spent represented a high proportion of a labourer's wage. One Croyland addict bought 40 pills a day at a cost of his entire income – two shillings.

Buying opium became an errand for children. In later life one recalled, "I went into a chemist's shop, laid a penny on the counter. The chemist said 'The Best?'. I nodded. He gave me a pill box and took up the penny and so the purchase was completed without my having uttered a syllable."

The habit was all but universal; the Fenman sought – and who can blame him? – to escape a drab, colourless, painful and degrading existence by a short trip to dreamland where he was unconscious of everything save the strange visions. Those badly under the influence or resurfacing after a 'fix' roared and bellowed like wild animals, giving rise to the nickname Fen Tigers.

I had a warm home and a job to go to when I left the fog-bound marsh, once denigrated by Thomas Hood as 'dreary, foggy, cloggy, boggy wastes'. The old-timers had no such escape and while the habit died out early in this century, they once indulged in drug-taking to an extent which would not have seemed out of place in latter day Colombia or South East Asia.

The Young Sportsman

*As a teacher and a sportsman, it was only natural
that John should take a keen interest in nurturing
the next generation of shooters. The articles in
this section trace both his own development
as a shooter and also the rites of passage
that will be familiar to so many
young shooters.*

The Young Shot, 4 February 1982

In this article from 1982, John revels in the innocent delight in the sport that the young shooter enjoys.

I t sometimes strikes me as odd that end-of-season cock days see boys and shoot helpers occupying the pegs. It is very right and proper that those who have loyally helped to show sport during the year should themselves be given a chance to shoot and it does no harm to prove to beaters, in the most practical way, that driven pheasants, which looked so simple from their standpoint earlier in the year, are quite easy to miss. On a shooting day, most beaters are too polite and well-trained to pass audible comment on the performance of those Guns who are suffering the misery of an 'off' day. However, no one can regulate their thoughts and quite clearly, the reflection sometimes crosses their minds that they could possibly have done better, had they been a forward gun.

When their chance comes to shoot, it is invariably at the end of the season, often in bad weather and at that most difficult of targets, a late January cock pheasant. Such a bird is yards faster than its November counterpart and really takes some hitting. A gun in peak form and with a full season's covert shooting under his belt ought to have a reasonable chance at these fast, high and often wickedly curling birds, but surely it is unfair to expect someone who rarely has the opportunity to shoot driven game to make any sort of showing at them.

To believe that would just be to show how wrong you were. Despite cold logic suggesting otherwise, one may often see mere slips of lads, barely out of the cradle, nobbling these birds with an assured and easy grace which makes the guv'nor blink. What it must be to possess limbs which are still lithe and supple and a head uncluttered with conflicting advice on how to shoot and a few decades of inconclusive and confusing experiences to go with it.

How many shooters have indelible childhood memories of their first Boxing Day or end-of season cock shoot? To the youngster and the beginner alone belong those bitter-sweet pre-shoot nerves, that conflict of desires – that all the birds fly over him and that nothing comes near him to expose his fearful ineptitude. How he wishes that the fast approaching cock would swerve and fly over a neighbour, and yet how deep is his disappointment when it actually does so. Not for him the 'coffee housing' with a neighbour at his peg during the 'boring' period of waiting for something to happen. Many emotions will afflict him, but boredom will not be ameng them

The waiting time is fraught with pent up emotions, not least of which are concern about his appearance and the hearty wish that he may not make an ass of himself, display conduct which might be remotely construed as dangerous or transgress the unwritten and complex etiquette which governs a shooting day. As for the shooting itself, how deep is his misery should he miss, how euphoric his joy when he scores. In my experience, a few butterflies in the tummy do no harm to the performance – quite the contrary. That injection of adrenalin can work wonders and for this reason, and also because the Fates are sometimes pricked by a sense of justice, the lad is usually able to kill at least one pheasant during the day.

How great then is his triumph: how keen the urge to rush out straight away and bag the bird lest it makes a miraculous recovery and head for the ditch, never to be seen again. How stern is the will-power which restrains him and causes him to wait until the drive is over. When the whistle blows, he is faced with another mental conflict. Should he run and get it now before it is lost from sight and carelessly tossed with a handful of other birds into the anonymity of the game cart? To wait for the picker-up might be the proper thing to do and would also suggest that you are no newcomer to the art of killing high pheasants. To display over-eagerness at a single bird down might be too blatantly to reveal your status as a beginner.

By a simple subterfuge, he manages to get his hands on the bird, either by strolling up casually, but just fast enough to beat a roving Labrador to the draw, or by taking it from the picker-up on some pretext or other. Once he has it, he strokes its feathers and examines it minutely, hoping to find his pellets in the forward half before he surrenders it reluctantly to the game cart. Before relinquishing it, he makes sure that as many people as possible have seen it in his hand – we are all human, and it was great to be young. Dare one whisper that even some comparative elders are not above hanging onto a brace of birds for longer than seems absolutely necessary. When the end of the day arrives, he swears that he can recognise his bird from among three score of others and, if given the opportunity, that is the one he will take home with him.

How hard a kind host tries to put the novice in the way of some shooting. He is not averse to juggling the pegs or chopping and changing quite shamelessly. His motives are the best, but experience should have told him that one may never win at that sort of game. Place anyone where he is likely to get a shot and the birds which usually stream over that position suddenly choose to avoid it and fly past some other peg which they normally eschew. Generally speaking, it is best to let everyone take his chance with the rest and, at the end of the day, it often turns out that the boy has had just as much or as little shooting as he would have done if the host had run himself ragged sorting out the likeliest places.

It is good to see the bright faces and shining eyes of lads out on their first 'proper' day and somehow, we feel able to share their pleasure and remind ourselves of our days of innocence. Sadly, repetition tends to dull the appetite and many Guns who do more than their share of driven shooting find that the magic and eager anticipation of boyhood fade all too soon and are lost for ever. In the end, they tend to spend as much time at the covertside socialising as shooting and, especially annoying to keepers, not being alert or maybe not even present when an early bird flies over their peg. To the young shot, every moment wasted over lunch is a matter for fretting impatience, whereas some old hands are never averse to taking an extra five minutes.

There are some happy, blessed men and women to whom the pleasures of a sporting day remain fresh and pristine, no matter how many years they have spent in the field. I am lucky to count some among my friends and they have the happy gift of approaching each occasion with the same lusty enthusiasm of a boy out for the first time. To shoot with such happy folk is a real pleasure, and their very presence seems to rekindle one's own waning fires.

Such a man, I guess – for I never knew him – was the late Noel 'Tim' Sedgwick, former editor of *Shooting Times*. A lady at my school kindly brought one of Tim's books to show me. It had been presented by the author to her father. To my delight, there appeared on the flyleaf a long dedication to his friend, Mr Lewsey, part of which reads, 'My own first experience of keepering was when I drove round with old Mr Keeper Lewsey, buying up hens eggs at 25 for a shilling to feed to the pheasant chicks. Since those days I have been a keeper over 3,000 acres and have now degenerated into writing about the profession! One of the things I remember best about your family, Harry, was your uncle's red tie! Good luck, a long life, plenty of wallop and may we meet again soon. Tim'.

Not for nothing did Tim write a book called *The Young Shot*, for there, surely was a man who maintained his youthful and fresh approach to all his sports, especially shooting, until the end of his days.

A Christmas Goose, 26 November 1981

Recounting one of his earliest shooting exploits, in this article from 1981 John demonstrated just how indelibly momentous events can etch themselves on an impressionable young mind.

I shot my first ever goose on Boxing Day and every Christmas I allow myself a nostalgic wallow as I recall the occasion. I can see his head mounted on a shield and gazing reproachfully down upon me as I write. His beady eye which seems to hold that faintly censorious expression has little enough cause to rebuke me. He was a fine, old bird who had lived the anserine equivalent of three score years and 10 and he it was who, in a moment of absent-mindedness, led his nine companions over the clump of frost-rimed Norfolk reed wherein I crouched.

I nearly did not go. Never had the bed seemed warmer as I peeped through the curtains at a sky that was clear and at stars which glittered hard and sharp like diamonds on a Hatton Garden, black velvet tray. A clear moon lit the roof tops and threw back a cold, ghostly reflection from the powdering of snow which two degrees of frost had turned to the consistency of powdered glass. No fowler would have blamed me had I snuggled back down between the covers and gone back to sleep like a Christian boy. Two thoughts kept me on my feet: one; I reflected that often in the past I had nearly not turned out, yet gone, and been justified in my decision: two; I was already out of bed and the hardest part of the early rising was over.

My bike skidded perilously on the frozen puddles, but at last I was safely at the marsh wall, sliding to a halt in the lee of some derelict farm buildings and concealing my machine in one of them where a broken-down Suffolk wain stood. Booted and armed with a long, brown-barrelled, single, magnum twelve, I stood shivering and felt the bite of frozen air in my nostrils. Ajax, my dog of the day who had already run two good miles behind me, skittered and danced, a pale ghost in a monochrome landscape.

I heard the distant bark of a dog on a lonely farm; a mallard quacked gently and a wigeon whistled. It was time to go, tinkling and crunching through filigrees of ice left by receding floodwater and as delicate as Nottingham lace. Every so often I would stop, hiss the dog to silence, hold my breath and listen intently before plodding onwards.

At last I came to one of my favourite spots, two miles up the marsh where a half-rotted gatepost leaned dangerously over some feathery reeds. An open stretch of water lay beyond it, now an ice-girt pool with a patch of open water in its middle. It looked as black as a puddle of ink beneath a half moon which swam through wisps of cloud as white as the cleanly-cut segment of an apple. With a splash and a grunt of alarm, a string of mallard sprang from the water and became instantly invisible against the star-studded sky.

I waded out cautiously with my six decoys. The water was not deep but I did not care to slip and suffer a ducking on a morning such as that. My decoys were family heirlooms, hardy veterans, paintless and chipped but they had seen many a duck killed over them and some, judging from the pellet holes from amongst them, and that long before I was born. They provided the reassuring black blobs on the water which incoming fowl might expect to see.

I draped some brown, frosted grass, flotsam from an earlier flood, onto the rushes slightly to thicken my cover. Even behind this flimsy screen I must have made a fearful, black figure hunched there in the gloom. Hopefully, when seen from ducks' eye view, I would not have been so conspicuous. Ajax's quivering bulk shivered at my knee; we both scanned the skies like old-time air raid wardens. The gun barrel felt blisteringly cold and the frost began to seep into my bones; ears and nose lost all feeling. I rubbed these extremities to restore the dull ache which proved they were still alive.

My hand was still in the act of massaging my ear when there was a flicker of wings and a silvery whistle across a pale dawn. A small knot of wigeon flashed across the curtain of cloud, vanished, reappeared and, with a whoosh, there they were on the water. My decoys seemed suddenly to have increased and multiplied. All at once, the real birds distinguished themselves; they relaxed and like clockwork toys began preening and dibbling. The nearest cock was not ten yards away, he put up his head and whistled with surprising loudness, 'wheeeooo...

wheeeooo…' Ajax's eyes stood out like the proverbial chapel hat pegs as we both gazed, spellbound at this enchanting little cameo.

The sun had now edged above the rim of the far bank and the Christmas cake landscape lost some, but not all, of its ghostliness. Two mallard passed, a very possible chance on my left. As I peered around at them and half-shifted the gun barrel, my wigeon sprang and flew with a whistle and a growl. My finger was on the trigger, but I did not fire. To have broken the solemn stillness of the scene would have been like whistling in church, an unwarranted sacrilege by an unwelcome intruder. I left the picture undisturbed but vowed to return when the gales swept the marshes and roared in the withy beds – proper fowling weather when the atmosphere was less supercharged. In those conditions I could knock down wigeon with an untroubled mind, but not at Christmas-tide when they had settled so trustingly close to me.

What about that goose? To that I am coming, but the story, like all good tales, keeps its twist until the final paragraphs. I was tramping back along the marsh track, ready for a snipe or one of our little, wild marsh pheasants, should one show, and I heard a distant bugling in the sky. There, far away and as steady as a constellation, flew a line of ten geese. How distant and untouchable they seemed; if only they would come over and give me half a chance at them. Not much hope of that. By their height and steadiness of flight, they knew just where they were going and were hardly likely to fly near me, one tiny dot on miles of untenanted marshland.

But that is exactly what they did. For no reason that I could identify, those whitefronts turned at right-angles, lost height and, still going strong and not intending to land, made directly for me. Had I myself flown up and guided them, they could not have flown over that opportune clump of reed behind which I had sunk with greater precision.

Ajax sat, good as gold, where I had dropped him, stock still in the open but his light coat blending with the icy tussocks. On and on came the birds. Surely I would miss, might they turn at this last moment and save me the humiliation and agony of muffing such a chance? They would not. The gun found the shoulder, finger the trigger while the eyes ranged through that leading, wide black shape; forward…

forward... forward... bang! There seemed to be an appreciable pause, just long enough for the heart to sink, the brain to say, 'missed', and the mind to beg for a second chance, but it was all right. There was a 'phruttt' of pellets striking pinions and, suddenly shrunken and aimless, my bird was falling for what seemed a full minute but was probably three seconds, and it thumped into the frosty grass with complete and exhilarating finality.

The head of that aged whitefront, admiral of the skein, mounted proudly on his shield, is the only stimulus I require to bring back that day with complete recall. Does not much of our love of fieldsports stem as much from what we remember as from what we do?

Enter Rosy, 18 February 1982

The acquisition of a first ferret is a seminal moment in any budding sporstman's career – in this article from 1982, John introduced readers to Rosy, his son David's rabbiting sidekick.

We took delivery at the last Game Fair. She came in a stout wooden box lined with hay and with a supermarket, vacuum-packed tray of rump steak as travelling rations. Clearly this was a ferret of good, if expensive, tastes. She was only a scrap of a thing, about the size of a weasel, and she divided her time equally between pirouetting and whirling round the box and lying fast asleep, dead to the world, paws tucked under chin and giving off little ferrety snores of contentment.

She travelled home in comfort and took over the palatial hutch which had been designed for her reception with five star comfort in mind. A hay-filled bedroom, large open space with sawdust underfoot, a juicy bone hanging from the ceiling, good supply of water and a stockpile of sparrows in the freezer seemed to have covered every possible need. Rosy explored every nook and cranny of this ferret's Taj

Mahal, giving her undivided attention to every wood shaving until the excitement of discovery and exploration gave way to an overwhelming drowsiness so that, in the middle of a private game, she would disappear into her boudoir and collapse into instant slumber.

In the morning, she greeted the new day as a miracle and would complete a tour of inspection to make sure that nothing had been moved or stolen during the night. Breakfast was a plump starling or sparrow, none of this bread and milk nonsense – ferrets are meat eaters and should be fed accordingly. She took the proffered bird with a speed and flash of white teeth which frightened the nervous spectator, but she rarely caught a finger by mistake. In no time, there was little left of her meal save a few scattered feathers.

Rosy was allowed into the house and loved romping round the room, laying ambush in the waste paper basket, running along the mantelpiece, dislodging a row of ornaments which fell like a toppling row of dominoes. She loved playing tag and, chittering with delight as the chase gained momentum, she would race ahead to a new vantage point, be it behind a sofa cushion or under a pile of mending. Winter sports were a special favourite and the snow offered an entirely new dimension to life. She believed that this gleaming white expanse had been created entirely for her benefit and treated it as a stage for a ferret ballet. She would leap, roll, twist, turn and then crouch motionless, inviting us to shower her with snow, the impact of the frozen particles inevitably triggering off another series of entrechats.

Rosy is the sole property and responsibility of my 12-year-old David, but her winning ways have made her something of a family favourite and we spend far too much time playing with her and organising our lives to make sure that she and the dogs never meet. She has given the air rifle a new meaning and purpose in life. I have never allowed random shooting at spar rows and starlings on the grounds that one should never shoot anything one is not going to use. This ruling has been rationalised by the growing appetite of Rosy and some selective Pot-hunting is now permitted. The larder remains full, while marksmanship steadily improves.

Life is not all play, and Rosy joined us as a working member of the family, not the senior bread-winner, perhaps, but one who was expected to make a contribution from time to time. As the winter wore on, we decided that it was time that Rosy saw the inside of a rabbit-hole. David had done his homework which started with long periods spent at the Pugs and Drummers stand, the reading and re-reading of Fred Taylor's book until the pages were worn through and even a close interrogation of the great man himself. Nets had been obtained; we bought some rather nasty nylon ones but then kind friends donated some much better ones, homemade with proper cord and with lovely, hand-whittled hazel pegs.

We already had a genuine Norfolk pole rabbiting spade, any number of knives and a bag in which to carry our bits and pieces. We even had a bleeper and a good box in which to carry Rosy to and from the scene of operations. Surely, no small jill ferret was ever so well supported and, quite clearly, the local rabbits were in for a nasty surprise. For all our preparations, there loomed in our minds one large, unnamed If. We had become very attached to Rosy and there was the unspoken dread that she might vanish into some labyrinthine warren, never to return. We had no big hob with which to drive her off a kill in a blind ally, and so we had to be selective as to holes. Those in hedge bottoms or in tree roots were out, as were buries which had numerous exits and entrances.

The ideal, of course, was a three holer, well out in a flat field, snag-free, easy digging, simple and quick to net but with no risk of losing the ferret. Easier said than found, for modern farmers love not the coney, especially when he sets up home among his beloved crops. As it is, he is quick enough with a polythene sack in the hole and a tin of cymag in the hedge bottoms and banksides. Such specific requirements in size, location and amenability of buries were not as restricting as one might imagine. We were not intending to set up as rabbit dealers; one, or at best a couple, would be quite enough for us and probably more than sufficient for an unentered, fat little jill the likes of Rosy.

The first outing was a blank. The gas man had done his stuff to deadly effect and his hawk eye seemed not to have missed the smallest hole. The expedition was not a complete failure, as Rosy learned that she was expected to go down the hole to see what was in there, and after a little coaxing, she seemed to get the hang of it. It was just another variation of a game to her. A day later, 'acting on information received',

David went with a school friend to a spinney just up the road. There they found and netted a compact four holer down which Rosy popped like a veteran. After a minute or so, a rabbit shot out of the bolt hole which the boys had found and covered. After a short struggle, during which it was touch and go who would end up the victor, the rabbit was bonked on the head, Rosy was retrieved, and the expedition returned down the high street in triumphal procession.

A 'first' can only happen once, and each one is an occasion to be savoured. Never again in his lifetime will that lad bolt his first rabbit with his own first ferret, and so there was due celebration and rejoicing. The next outing was up to the rape field from which a cloud of at least 1,000 pigeon lifted at our approach. There were plenty of holes in the hedge bottom but we stuck to our rule and found some prefab granny-flat burrows out in the field. Luckily I came along as chauffeur/digger, for my services in the latter capacity were soon to be required. A long shallow dig down a blind ally eventually produced Rosy and her second victim where they were jammed together in a dead end. Fired by this success, we decided to risk a small bury at the end of the thorn hedge. We netted the holes and Rosy slid down one like a lazy, myopic snake. She was gone for what seemed an age; anxiety grew. Then there came an angry chittering from below ground and a large brown rat slipped out through the net and into the hole next door.

There was still no sign of Rosy but a further burst of sneezing and sounds of a subterranean affray preluded her sudden emergence with blood streaming from a cut on her nose. The rats had clearly got the better of her so we decided to call it a day.

By next morning her duelling scar had healed and she was once more her playful self, living in a dream of her own existence, innocently giving affection for kindness received and, despite her experience, believing the world to be one enormous playground.

Old Heads, 26 January 1984

With one geriatric dog and one tyro sportsman taking his first shots, this Country Gun column from 1984 shows how hard a parent sometimes must work to propogate a shared passion.

I am convinced that Drake, my 10-year-old Labrador has, in his old age, become a hypochondriac – and a crafty one at that. In his day, he was a lion in the chase, bold but affectionate and on countless occasions he filled the bag, earning the nickname among our friends of The Bag-Filling Dog. Times changed, its winged chariot caught up with him and suddenly, he aged. A muzzle which on his eighth birthday was jet black was first touched with frost and then covered with snow 12 months later. He took to waddling about rheumatically, affected a limp, dawdled behind on walks and grew shameless in extorting sympathy from those who knew him no better. I would try to hurry him up as he lagged behind, making me late for school, but he shot me such a reproachful glance that I grew too easy on him.

His deafness comes and goes in a manner surely unbeknown to veterinary science. Call him off a running cock and his affliction is sore to behold; summon him to his dinner or allow his feeding bowl so much as to tap against the door and he comes like a corpulent rocket to the trough. Grow exasperated with his interminable static investigation of an interesting smell, stoop for a clod of earth to throw to gain his attention and again he anticipates by leaping into action, proving that the corner of watery eye was on me all the time.

His place in the shooting field has been taken by a young thruster, but on half days, holidays, or for a potter round after a pheasant on a frosty afternoon, he is brought out of semi-retirement and, again, his limp suddenly vanishes, and he prances around like a puppy. I have often claimed that shooting has therapeutic properties and there is the proof. In the field, his progress through the brambles is slower than it was three years ago, but just as flamboyant and more thorough. The whole bush shakes wildly as though with an earthquake; leaves fall, small birds fly out, there is a grunting, wheezing sound and his face, festooned with old man's beard and burrs, with a three-inch scratch on his nose, squeezes out of a rabbit run on the far side. Sometimes the face is preceded by the eruption of a crafty old pheasant which thought it was safe, but just as often, the bird is already clamped into Drake's mouth, having been emphatically pegged in the heart of the prickles.

At the other end of a shooting career my lad David is still keen on his gun, due largely, I suspect, to my 'softly softly' policy. It is a great mistake to force the pace and take things too fast. An interest in shooting can be a delicate bloom, easily killed with too much watering: leave it be and little by little, it will grow. Over-fertilise it and it outruns its strength, flourishes briefly and then dies. His favourite is duck shooting so, as a reward for a good school report, I took him down to the Ouse washes to see if we could find him a shot. The Great Level was bone dry, grazed hard by sheep and devoid of duck.

We stood by the flood bank in a bitter wind which had pellets of sleet on its breath; every so often, a volley of it would rattle on our upturned hoods. There was a general quacking far and near from the river, so what wildfowl there were had wisely roosted in the lee of the bank. I had stood in this very spot in these exact conditions with precisely the same intentions, 30 years before.

I must have been better at bank crawling in those days, for today the duck were up and away in the quarter light while the East was little more than a smudge of pale grey. A dozen parties of from six to 20 mallard came down river, making height rapidly; it was clear that other fowlers had been trying the same old trick and had made them suspicious. One lot did seem to be a reasonable chance and we both fired but failed to connect.

So much for the duck flight and the dawn now showed us a completely duckless scene. We set off, walking the rough bank for one of the wild marsh pheasants, but they too were not at home and we found none. The locals had probably been giving them a hard time. A lone greylag and then a cormorant flew at great height down the wash. We zig-zagged back, stalking the duck ponds and the old willow holt, but it seemed that there was not a shootable bird left in the parish.

As a last resort, I sent David to walk the edge of the river beside a dense bed of osiers. Memory told me that any pheasant flushed from it would fly that way. I told him to listen to the dogs and me crashing about and keep going, slightly ahead of us, ready for anything which might come his way. I set off through the jungle, the dogs needing no encouragement to hunt the nettle stems, hogweed and water docks. We had worked down about three-quarters of the holt when there came a distant shot and a cry of, "I've got it!", and then another shot. What could it mean? I struggled out into the daylight to join David to find that my worst fears had been realised. A canny old cock had slipped silently out in front of him. He had fired and dropped it on the far bank where it had recovered and run off over the top and out of sight.

It was a two-mile walk to the nearest bridge and back to the other side of where we stood; the dogs had not marked the fall. Kenzie went over easily and eagerly enough, but I could not persuade him to go out of sight over the bank. Drake eyed the water, me, and then the water again. "You must be joking," he looked, but I hardened my heart and got him in at last. He wallowed across like a hippo and hauled himself out on the far bank. He went straight out over the flood wall and thus gave Kenzie the general idea of my requirements. Drake came back a couple of times for fresh directions, but Kenzie seemed to have gone for good: I should be so lucky!

We waited impatiently, fingers tightly crossed and then, Drake, still empty-mouthed, slowly topped the far bank; he had been our best hope, but then 'Oh joy!' another canine face, like Chad, demurely rose over the ridge, its muzzle enhanced by a very old and very angry cock pheasant. David and I did a short war dance among the osiers: all Kenzie's crimes (and Heaven knows, they are legion), were forgiven on the spot, but later I was plagued by the unkind thought that maybe old Drake had found the bird and, out of sight beyond the bank, dastardly Kenzie had stolen it from him. The pheasant was, I guess, about the same age as the boy, with scimitar spurs, each feather stuck into its skinny chest like glue, a tail 18 inches long and a beak like a condor's. How long, I wonder, had he lurked in that wild place, sliding low and silent over the bank each morning and wise to all the tricks; fired at and missed how many times? Whatever the answers, it was the right one to shoot and the perfect bird for a boy who had never in his life shot a cock pheasant. Calloo Callay! For me, the big question was whether

Kenzie or Drake had run it down and, as the American films tend to say, 'That, we will never know'.

Suitable photographs were taken but there was more to come, for I was then mindful of a muddy ditch out in the Fen which had, in the past, served me well after a blank flight; it was worth seeing if it was still a likely spot. I drove to the place through the mud and parked the Subaru two fields away. At that very moment, right on cue, three mallard flew in from afar and confidently dropped straight down into the ditch; clearly, some duck were already there to draw them in. With a world-weary glance I noted the particular clump of bleached grass which marked the spot. One does not shoot the same dyke for 30 years without learning at least the basics.

We lugged our boots, each one now coated with 10lb of Fen mud, up the barley drill and there we were, in line with the place. I gave a short and belated pep talk: "Shoot them in the head; take your time pick, your bird. Remember, they will be rising." That was enough for one go and, with mounting excitement, we crept the last few yards to the clump of grass. Thirty mallard sprang as one, paddles dripping, hoarsely quacking. As I raised my gun, I saw, from the corner of my eye, a drake collapse. So much for 'taking his time', or was I getting slow? I took a measured right and left and Drake struggled over the drain four times to pick four birds, two each.

It is hard to say who was the more pleased, the boy with his first cock pheasant and his first right and left at anything, or his father who secretly thanked his gods that at least he had been able to bag his two!

Boy's eye view, 13 February 1986

You want your children to understand and value the sport that they take part in – in this article from 1986, John writes of the triumph and pride of a boy's first bird.

In the dying moments of an otherwise unremarkable shooting season, and just when it seemed it was too late for miracles, there came out of the grey a sudden flash of coleur de rose. Wrinkled family retainers gathered respectfully in the gunroom at Humphreys Towers and there was not a dry eye to be seen as, their gnarled hands trembling with emotion, they raised their glasses to toast the occasion of the young master's first pheasant.

No. 2 son Peter is serving his apprenticeship in the shadow of his brother and has shot duck, pigeon and rabbits but on the odd occasion when I have put him within range of a pheasant, he has made a hopeless mess of it, firing where the bird has been rather than where it is going. This became a matter of increasing frustration since, in most things, he tends to be blessed with more than his share of luck but, at the end of a second season of hard trying, that first pheasant seemed as remote a prospect as ever.

Then, on beaters' day, he found himself with two others bringing in a boundary dyke with instructions to shoot any cocks which might break back. Halfway down a single cock, pushed out by a springer, turned into the stiff wind and struggled back past us towards the river. At 15 yards range and virtually hovering, it was not what you might call an impossible target. Peter took deliberate aim and fired – a clean miss! A pause and he fired again and this time the bird came clattering down. Hooray! I was pumping the boy by the hand and showering blessings on his head when there came a warning cry from Trevor. Even before Kenzie could get to it, the pheasant had recovered, and sailed off towards the horizon.

Merely stunned, by gad! No more stunned than we as, open mouthed, we watched the first pheasant so nearly in the bag, diminishing into the distance. I marked it down in a lonely coppice and nobly offered to go back and look for it, leaving the others to carry on. I trudged away, worked out the spinney and flushed and shot the one cock pheasant in it which may or may not have been the one. I took it back, but it seemed a muted and unsatisfactory effort for a first pheasant and not really admissible in the strictly kept score-books of our consciences.

Later in the day all was put to rights in a way which even the keenest recording angel would have accepted without a quibble. Peter was one of three Guns sent to stand at the end of a long shelter-belt. He found himself next to 'G', one of our senior Guns towards whom only suicidal pheasants will fly, for 'G' has cobra-swift, deadly reactions to anything within range, irrespective of over which peg it happens to be flying. It was just as well for Peter that on this occasion the sun was in 'G's' eyes. A single cock rocketed up from the tangled briars and flew at poplar height the length of the belt. Peter raised his gun, fired one shot and the bird threw back its head and fell emphatically and exhilaratingly dead, splashing down into the ditch.

So, dear reader, can you wonder at the rejoicing and the drinking of healths, the snapping of camera-shutters, back-thumping and careful marking of the unlucky bird to distinguish it from the rest of the bag at the end of the day? I envied him the experience. My own first pheasant I carried home rather than risk crumpling it in the bag and the possible bending of its tail. I showed it to all the neighbours; I exposed a whole reel of film in the family Brownie. I stroked its feathers, studied them, plucked some especially gaudy ones and glued them in my diary. I hung it for too long rather than pluck it and spoil its looks, gloated shamelessly over its Persian rug colours, felt its hard, nutty, curved beak, deliberately pricked my finger and winced at its sharp spurs. Eventually and reluctantly it was feathered and eaten with a relish more appropriate to lark tongues in aspic than a rather stringy Fen pheasant.

I reckon I got a fair mileage from that bird but what happens now? A shot pheasant is brought to hand, either retrieved by a dog, produced by a picker-up or gathered with your own fair hand. With barely a second glance at it and almost as if resentful of the intrusion, we toss it onto a pile of the slain by the verge, turn our backs on it and resume our interrupted conversation. Where has gone that boyhood eagerness and freshness which once made us want to mark the bird which we shot, to feast it with the eye, to enjoy such an intense experience at every possible level and savour it to the full?

It was for a similar reason that we old hands with wistful looks in our eyes watched Peter stroking his first pheasant. How we wished that, for a moment, we too could have recaptured the magic moment of our own first good shot, not only recaptured it but retained it, so that every bird shot and every day out became as fresh and shining as that first ever one.

Sadly, we come to confuse quantity with quality. We have concluded that because it is exciting to shoot a pheasant, to shoot ten is ten times as exciting and therefore, it must follow, that to shoot 1,000 is 1,000 times as exciting. How often must we experience it before we recognise the philosophy – if philosophy it is – to be false, bottomless and only a further manifestation of Man's greed? It leads to a shooting man tossing aside his shot birds with a jest and in a manner which not only shows scant respect for the quarry but indicates that a proper, primitive lust for the hunt – one of the oft-voiced justifications for fieldsports – is fading.

Both my sons are passing their shooting apprenticeship and I confess myself proud of their progress. Quite as important as marksmanship, quarry identification and even safety (for anyone can learn them given time and a good coach), is it to retain a sportsmanlike attitude to this grand pursuit of ours, to try to preserve, despite pressures to do otherwise, a boy's fresh delight at each day out. It is not impossible, for I can think of at least three elderly sportsmen who still have that boyish enthusiasm which most of us left behind when we shed our school caps. Still they stroke a pheasant as though marvelling at it for the first time; still they rejoice over the glint of a stippled trout as if they neared their seventh rather than their 70th birthdays.

If I can somehow bequeath to David and Peter that approach I will rest easy under the sod – far more easily than if I had trained the most efficitient pheasant-butcher, fishmonger, competitive bag-filler, hit-man or Hot Shot clay-shatterer in the whole green land of England.

Lucky Jim, 23 July 1987

Isn't it just the case that some people are blessed with good fortune? When it's your own young son who's the fortunate one, that blessing is even more galling – as this Country Gun column from 1987 shows.

Napoleon asked his prospective new generals one key question at their interviews. It was not if they were good tacticians, natural leaders of men or masterly handlers of cavalry in the field; he asked them simply whether or not they were lucky and, depending on their answer, he hired or rejected them. Whether or not we manufacture and earn our own luck is a matter for a philosophical debate inappropriate here, but the fact is that some people could tumble headfirst into a mound of pheasant droppings and emerge in a new suit, clutching a bunch of asparagus and a jar of Beluga caviar.

I often suspect that No. 2 son, Peter, falls firmly into this category. This is no proud father boasting, and I rely on readers to let me know if they are fed up with him and his exploits, but his elder brother and father had to work, sweat and struggle to strike even a share of his success. Shooting fathers who are lucky enough to have shooting sons are doubly blessed, for they relive their own early experiences, rejuvenate a view of the sporting life which may be beginning to flag and rejoice far more in the success of a novice than they do at a good shot of their own. For all that, I could happily strangle him at times, especially when he begins to advise me on where I am going wrong.

No. 2 sat in a row of anglers on a dreary bank on a Fenland cut; dug arrow-straight by the Romans it ran from one horizon to another, no more than a yard deep; as soon try to catch a fish in his mother's washing tub, I thought.

His dead roach, carefully impaled on a paternoster which was old when my father had it, lay on the mud, indistinguishable from the other dead roach of his fellow piscators stationed at cricket pitch length intervals to the left and right of him. After a half-hour wait, the gaudy *Fishing Gazette* pike bung he bought in a jumble sale bobbled, slid away, stopped, jiggled, paused and then glided off in a slow and stately manner. He flicked over the bale arm, took a good grip on my best salmon-spinning rod and struck as I have seen deck hands strike on tuna boats in the South Pacific.

There was an eruption in the depths as a great tail broke surface and a likely enough fish set off upstream as though rushing to catch a train. After a series of plunging runs, boring dives and startling threshes dangerously close to the reeds, a yard and a bit of green, blotched pike slid over the rather inadequate landing net held by a small boy from 4B. The fight had taken a good ten minutes.

She lay in stately dignity on the rough grass with her liquid jewel of a stricken deer eye full of all the sorrows of too much worldly wisdom, the lean raking chops like old cartoons of Uncle Sam; and when she eased open those fearful jaws, serried ranks of teeth upon teeth, plates of bone covered with thorny cat claws all contained by a wicked, picket fence of pearly, needle spikes caused the ring of crowding spectators to draw back an involuntary step in alarm.

Camera and scales had been left at home, so guess who did the return trip to collect both? She swung the needle round to 181/21b of sinister beauty, a green widow with who could guess at how many suitors eaten? Those sad eyes gave nothing away.

She glided back into the green ripples, horrified tiddlers showering out of her way like handfuls of rice flung at a wedding as she slanted down towards her old lie by the flags, but the minnows need not have worried as, for the time being, she had lost her appetite.

Five minutes later he landed a 'masterful gurt owd eel' as they say in the Fen country and, rolled in egg and breadcrumbs, it made a good breakfast next morning, especially when accompanied by two fried eggs and four rashers of best back.

I wouldn't mind, but he does this sort of thing all the time and easy success is not the best way to learn the hard lessons. Last year he went piking twice and caught one of the best pike on the Cam that year and that on a homemade spoon. On shooting days he inevitably finds himself in the best spot; once he got confused and pulled the front trigger three times at a flush of teal, realised his mistake, pulled the other one in a rush, and a second bird miraculously fell. We walk in line towards a sunken dyke and guess in front of whom the only two mallard in it for five miles choose to lumber skywards. It's enough to make you spit!

Off to a Zabala star, 6 April 2006

How much value can you get out of one gun? As it turns out, an awful lot if that gun has kick-started the shooting careers of dozens of young sportsmen and women, as this Country Gun column from 2006 shows.

I n the catalogue of the world's great shotguns, the name Zabala might not make it into the top ten; it is not a moniker that springs to the lips when the talk comes round to fine engraving and French walnut. I mean no insult – it is horses for courses. The dray horses that come from the Zabala Spanish stable have their place along with the race horses bred by Mr Purdey, Mr Boss and both Mr Hollands.

I bought one 27 years ago, for £40, brand new, a side-by-side 20-bore, straight hand stock, non-ejector, a good old plain Jane with a safety catch like a gooseberry. A while ago this gun featured in my *Shooting Times* column and readers might like to know that it is still doing the business initiating young shooters. It was bought for No. 1 son, who was tiring of the air rifle. We did not fall into the trap of getting him a .410. Though the little gun has its uses and is advocated for beginners, I say a child wants a lot of shot, open bores, a stock that fits and, most important of all, success.

Many youngsters escape the pitfall of the .410 only to be turned off shooting by being given an adult's gun. They have to stretch to reach the triggers, the barrels are too long, the recoil knocks them about and they never hit anything. "Shame to cut the stock on grandpa's gun but don't worry, son, you'll grow into it," says cheery Uncle Bob, as the lad rubs his shoulder, mops a bloody nose and gazes ruefully at the umpteenth missed bird. By the time he is big enough it is too late and Johnny has gone off to watch football instead.

Having seen this all too often, I took the Zabala to Adrian Lemmon of Cambridge Gun Repairs, who cut down the stock by 3in, rebalanced it and opened the chokes to true and improved cylinder. I bought light loads of 7s and gave the boy his head under strict supervision. We followed the ancient code for heavy bags, namely open chokes, small shot and get in close. With that pattern at 20 yards, the shooter had the edge. Early success meant that he took to the sport and now, rising 36, he is as keen as ever – so thank you, Zabala. Had the Zabala been a Purdey I would not have desecrated the stock or fiddled with the chokes and every scratch and scrape would have brought tears to the eyes. After two seasons he grew out of it and while I kept the spare bit of stock so it could be reattached, I passed it on to No. 2 son who went through the same process. That gun shot pinkfooted geese, common snipe and everything between, all at comfortable range, as the pattern was good but short lived.

The Zabala's life after Peter was by no means over. I had no more sons coming through, but my friends did, and there she was, just waiting to initiate them, the perfect beginner's gun that fitted, no choke, enough shot to wallop things and little recoil. Other boys borrowed the Zabala, kept it for a year or so until they were hooked, then they outgrew it and passed it back. I wish I had kept a record of those who learned on it and shot their first pheasant, but it must be about 15 boys and one girl. That works out at about £2 per child.

The latest is nine-year-old Ben Jeacock, son of my friend Simon and grandson of Michael, a shooting pal of half a lifetime on the fen. The Zabala is getting a little worn and the blueing is fading – each of its custodians polished it assiduously, but the gun is sound and game for any number of young lads. Ben lives in a strict shooting household, is safer than some adults I know and can distinguish a grey partridge from a redleg. What a proud moment then, when all three took to the field to shoot together at the end of last season and prouder still when Ben shot his first cock pheasant. The Zabala still cuts the mustard when held true. I envied the lad his success, for don't we all recall how we felt with our own first? I met Ben's mother a month later and she told me that they had just eaten the bird and the lad was as proud as a cock pheasant with 15 hens.

My grandson Max, aged three, correctly identified a coal tit, a blue tit and a robin on his bird table, a feat that some adults find testing. It is my dream that one day he will aspire to the Zabala like his father before him, and if, like the Jeacocks, we are especially blessed, we will take to the field together. If he were as fortunate as Ben and shot his first pheasant with the gun his father christened so long ago, then indeed our cup would run over.

Forty quid well spent, wouldn't you say?

Valete

Country Gun, Shooting Times,
15 February 2012

Forty years after he first wrote for **Shooting Times,**
*the magazine published John Humphreys' final
weekly column, only a few days after his
death from cancer. It was a bittersweet
look at a life well-lived, and a fond
farewell to thousands of
friends.*

Dear reader-

I use the word in the singular because I see you all as individual friends as well as a great crowd of chums I might meet at a party. All this jollity I fear is to end. You may have noticed my last three or four offerings might have lacked some of their snap, wit and wisdom, along with containing the odd non sequitur.

To anyone who thinks this, I would say, just you try working a laptop while lying even more flat on your back than last time, with your chin jammed on its leading edge, your eyeballs swivelling downwards on their stalks, and elbows stuck out like two portions of a chicken dinner.

The fact is that my lovely and brave wife, Angela, has taken this from dictation. She, along with my family, has been a great prop to me through this difficult time. The truth is, old friend, my condition has deteriorated more swiftly than I could have imagined and last night I glanced down the valley of the shadow, although I seem to have made a remarkable recovery this morning, enabling me to dictate this sad missive.

So it is time to look back – and what a lot we have to look back on. Coveys of partridges spraying like bullets over Norfolk plantings; skeins of pinks clamouring out of a blood red dawn; rabbits pushed out of a hedge bottom by a spaniel/terrier combo; fen pheasants arcing over a blue fenland sky. We will have seen flickering snipe and woodcock, pigeons whirring into the beechmast or swinging over the rape, and if we are lucky, the ultimate challenge of grouse defying the contours. We must not forget the fish. Many a good trout has come to net and fine salmon have been grassed. Then there was a little desultory stalking and second-hand falconry, guinea fowl in Africa, wild boar in Germany, ducks in Cuba, Spanish partridge – to mention more would be a bore.

So all that remains is to wish you all a fond farewell, for *Shooting Times* was always my favourite magazine. It was a hefty deduction from my week's pocket money, especially when cartridges at 12/3d a box were taken into consideration. However, as my father enjoyed reading my copy and being a fair man with a larger income than mine, he decided that 'The Shooter' should be added to the family budget. It started a friendship that continued with dear old 'Fenman' in 1972, a friendship enhanced when Tony Jackson, my first editor, took a risk with me and made me 'weekly', warning me sardonically as he did so that 'you realise this means 52 articles a year, Humphreys'.

Since then we have had our ups and downs, but mostly it is a story of ups, and of many good friends made.

I can only wish you good sport and happy lives, and that you will continue to support our sporting bodies. As for me, it's a fond farewell, and if we are lucky we might meet again on a splendid pheasant shoot in the next world – as long as I'm not paying.